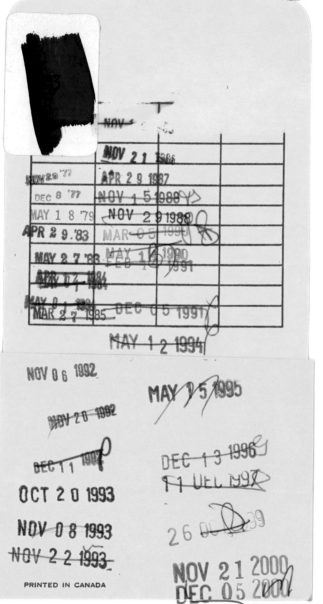

The Cold War

Random House Historical Issues Series

THE COLD WAR—
WHO IS
TO BLAME?

Random House

Preface

A major purpose of this series of pamphlets is to convince students in Western civilization courses that the essential task of a historian is not to collect dead facts but to confront live issues. The issues are alive because they arise out of the tensions that men have to face in every generation—tensions between freedom and authority, between reason and faith, between human free will and all the impersonal circumstances that help to shape our lives.

In order to achieve any sophisticated understanding of such matters, a student needs to read the views of great modern historians as they are set out in their own words. He needs to develop a measure of critical historical insight by comparing these often conflicting views with the source material on which they are based. He needs above all to concern himself with the great issues that have shaped the course of Western civilization and not with historical "problems" that are mere artificially contrived conundrums.

We believe that there are three major themes whose development and interplay have shaped the distinctive characteristics that set Western civilization apart from the other great historic cultures. They are the growth of a tradition of rational scientific inquiry, the persistence of a tension between Judaeo-Christian religious ideals and social realities, the emergence of constitutional forms of government. These three themes are introduced in the first pamphlets of the series. The reader will find them recurring in new forms and changing contexts throughout the rest of the pamphlets. We hope that in studying them he will come to a richer understanding of the heritage of Western civilization—and of the historian's approach to it.

Ithaca, 1968   BRIAN TIERNEY

DONALD KAGAN

L. PEARCE WILLIAMS

The Cold War—

Who Is To Blame?

CONTENTS

1 America's Responsibility ✓   4

FROM *The Cold War and Its Origins* BY D. F. FLEMING   4

2 The Development of the Cold War ✓   18

President Roosevelt's Letter to Marshal Stalin   18
FROM *Speaking Frankly* BY JAMES F. BYRNES   21
FROM *A Beginning for Sanity*
     BY NORMAN COUSINS AND THOMAS K. FINLETTER   22
FROM *The Forrestal Diaries*   24
FROM *United States Proposals for the International Control
     of Atomic Energy*   25
FROM *Winston Churchill's Speech at Fulton*   33
Message of the President to the Congress   37
Editorial from Izvestia   42
The European Recovery Program   44
FROM *President Beneš' Correspondence with the Presidium
     of the Communist Party*   47
North Atlantic Treaty   50

3 Russia's Responsibility ✓   55

FROM *A Diplomatic History of the American People*
     BY THOMAS A. BAILEY   55

4 A European View   67

FROM *A History of the Cold War* BY JOHN LUKACS   67

QUESTIONS FOR STUDY

1   In what ways do Fleming and Bailey disagree on the facts of the Cold War?

2   What was the part played by the Baruch plan in the Cold War?

3   Why did Russia reject it?

During the Second World War the United States, Great Britain, and the Soviet Union were allied in a fight for survival against the Axis powers. From the beginning there were differences in strategy, aims, and ideology, accompanied by mutual distrust. Nevertheless the alliance held together; at Teheran and Yalta conferences were held and joint plans made for the conduct of the war and for the shape of the peace to come. A United Nations organization was envisaged in which all would participate to maintain peace and harmony. But within a few years hopes for friendship and cooperation had been dashed and the world was divided into two hostile armed camps; the Cold War had begun. It is the aim of this chapter to investigate the problem of how this reversal came about.

4   *What was the beginning of the breach between Russia and the United States?*

5   *What is the importance of the coup in Czechoslovakia?*

6   *Compare the views of Fleming, Bailey, and Lukacs on the importance of the Truman Doctrine, the Marshall Plan, and NATO.*

1 America's Responsibility

*In the following selection D. F. Fleming presents the view
that the United States was largely responsible for the coming of the Cold War and establishes the nature of the
controversy.*

FROM *The Cold War and Its Origins*
BY D. F. FLEMING

THE CHRONOLOGY OF THE COLD WAR

THERE CAN BE NO REAL UNDERSTANDING of the Cold War unless
chronology is kept in mind. What came first? What was action and what
reaction? Not everything that came after a given act was due to that act, but
a later event could not be the cause of an earlier one.

Below are the principal events of the Cold War in the order in which
they occurred.

1 September 1938—Control of East Europe achieved by Hitler at Munich.
2 December 5, 1941 to February 4, 1942—State Department decisions not
to make any wartime agreements about Russia's western boundaries.
3 April 1942 to June 1944—The second front postponed. Peripheral war
conducted in Africa and Italy.
4 October 9, 1944—Churchill and Stalin agreed on spheres of influence in
the Balkans: Greece to Britain; Bulgaria and Rumania to Russia;
Yugoslavia 50–50.
5 December 3, 1944 to January 15, 1945—The British crushed the Greek
leftists in heavy fighting.
6 December 24, 1944 to May 14, 1945—Bulgarian purge trials executed
2000 rightists and imprisoned 3000.
7 March 29, 1944 to February 1945—Soviet armies occupied East Europe.

From *The Cold War and Its Origins, 1917–1960*, II (1961), 1038–51, by D. F. Fleming.
Reprinted by permission of Doubleday & Company, Inc., and George Allen & Unwin Ltd.,
London.

8 February 1945—The Yalta Conference conceded friendly governments in East Europe to Russia, but with free elections and a reorganization of the Polish Government.

9 March 6, 1945—Russia imposed a communist-led coalition in Rumania.

10 March 1945—Friction with Russia over German surrender negotiations in Italy.

11 April 12, 1945—Franklin D. Roosevelt's death, four months after Cordell Hull's resignation.

12 April 23, 1945—Truman's White House lecture to Molotov on the Polish Government.

13 July 17-25, 1945—The Potsdam Conference failed to alter Russian arrangements in East Europe.

14 August 6, 1945—The first American A-bomb upset the expected world strategic balance.

15 August 18, 1945—Beginning of the Byrnes-Bevin diplomatic drive to force free elections in East Europe.

16 September 1945—First Council of Foreign Ministers deadlocked over East Europe.

17 March 5, 1946—Churchill's Fulton speech demanded an Anglo-American preponderance of power against Russia, with reference to East Europe.

18 April 1946—Russian troops forced from Iran through the United Nations.

19 August 1946—Soviet demands upon Turkey for the return of two provinces and for a base in the Straits.

20 July to December 1946—Peace treaties for Italy, Hungary, Rumania, Bulgaria and Finland hammered out.

21 November 1946—The Republicans won control of the Congress, aided by charges of widespread communist infiltration in the United States.

22 Late December 1946—General relaxation and expectation of peace.

23 March 12, 1947—The Truman Doctrine, calling for the containment of the Soviet Union and communism.

24 March 23, 1947—Truman's order providing for the loyalty investigation of *all* government employees.

25 March to August 1947—The freely elected Smallholder's Party Government of Hungary disintegrated by communist pressure.

26 June 5, 1947—The Marshall Plan announced. Rejected by Russia August 2, 1947.

27 November 1947—The Cominform organized, uniting all the principal communist parties of Europe, including those of France and Italy.

28 January 22, 1948—A plan for a Western Union in Europe announced by Bevin.

29 February 25, 1948—A communist coup seized control of Czechoslovakia.

30 March 25, 1948—Western Union treaty signed. Devil theory address by President Truman.

31 June 28, 1948—Yugoslavia expelled by the Cominform. Received help from the West.

32 June 1948 to May 1949—The Berlin blockade.

33 March to August 1949—The signing and ratification of the North Atlantic Treaty creating NATO.

34 September 23, 1949—The first Soviet A-bomb hung the threat of total destruction over West Europe.

35 February 1, 1950—Drive for the H-bomb announced by Truman.

36 February 9, March 9 and 16, 1950—Acheson explained the policy of no negotiation with the Russian river of aggression until strength had been accumulated.

37 October 1948 to January 1950—The Chinese Nationalist armies captured or destroyed by the Communists.

38 February to May 1950—The first explosion of McCarthyism.

39 June 25, 1950—The outbreak of the Korean War.

40 September 12, 1950—The United States demanded the rearmament of Germany and began a vast rearmament.

41 October 1950—Having liberated South Korea, we decided to conquer the North Korean Republic.

42 February 1952—Acheson's Lisbon NATO arms goals overstrained our allies.

43 May to November 1952—Our allies escaped from control during the long American election campaign.

44 November 1952—The first American H-bomb exploded, on the ground.

45 March 6, 1953—The death of Stalin created uncertainty and a desire for relaxation in Russia.

46 May 11, 1953—Churchill repealed his Fulton address and called for an end of the Cold War on the basis of guaranteeing Russia's security in East Europe.

47 July 26, 1953—Korean cease-fire signed.

48 August 9, 1953—The first air-borne H-bomb achieved by Russia, and growing Russian air power brought the threat of incineration to all large American cities.

49 November 6, 1953—Ex-President Truman officially charged with knowingly harboring a communist spy.

50 May 1952 to January 1954—A growing realization that the world power struggle had become a stalemate.

51 April 22 to June 15, 1954—The crest of McCarthyism.

52 July 18-24, 1955—The First Summit Conference recognized the atomic arms stalemate and the inevitability of competitive coexistence.

53 February 15-20, 1956—Khrushchev's denunciation of Stalin accelerated a wave of reforms behind the iron curtain, relaxing police state controls and giving greater incentives to individuals.

54 March 7, 1956—President Eisenhower urged that we counter the threat to us "more by positive measures that people throughout the world will trust, than just by trying to answer specific thrusts."

55 October-November 1956—Revolution in Poland and Hungary against Soviet control and Communism.

56 November 1956—Attacks upon Egypt by Israel, France and Britain.

57 August 26, 1957—The first intercontinental ballistic rocket claimed by the Soviet Union.

58 October 4, 1957—The first of the increasingly heavy Sputniks demonstrated Russia's ability to lay down large pay-loads accurately across great distances.

59 April 1958—The pro-American Liberal Party ousted in Canada by the strongly nationalistic Conservatives.

60 May 1958—Vice President Nixon mobbed in Peru and Venezuela.

61 July 1958—Revolution in Iraq and the sending of American troops to Lebanon.

62 August-October 1958—The second Quemoy crisis, ending in China's defeat.

63 November 1958 to July 1959—The second Berlin crisis.

64 April 16, 1959—The resignation of Secretary of State John Foster Dulles.

65 September 1959—Khrushchev's visit to the United States, inaugurating President Eisenhower's effort to move toward making peace and ending the Cold War.

66 September-October 1959—A Soviet *Lunik* rocket hit the moon and another went around it relaying to earth pictures of its hidden side, emphasizing Russia's continued leadership in rocketry and the conquest of space.

67 November 16, 1959—Secretary of State Herter's appeal for keeping the great competition of our time with communism "within the bounds set by the conditions of co-survival."

68 December 1959—Eisenhower's eleven nation crusade for a new international climate and peace, climaxed by his statement to the Parliament of India on December 10 that the mistrusts, fixations and tensions that exist in the world "are the creations of Governments, cherished and nourished by Governments. Nations would never feel them if they were given freedom from propaganda and pressure."

69 October 1955 to May 1960—The Second Summit Conference frustrated by the steady erosion in the West of the expectation of serious negotiations about West Berlin and by the U-2 spy plane incident at Sverdlovsk.

70 June 16, 1960—President Eisenhower turned back from a visit to Japan by the inability of the Japanese Government to protect him from great hostile demonstrations.

It is of cardinal importance to remember that East Europe was given away not at Yalta but at Munich. Before that the curbing of Hitler might have cost the West the same territories which Hitler yielded to Russia. After

Munich the marching armies would grind back and forth across the face of Europe until the Red armies came to rest in Berlin and Vienna.

DECISIONS DURING THE WAR

This was not foreseen in the State Department as late as December 5, 1941 and February 1942 when the Atherton-Dunn memoranda reasoned that Stalin might not be able to recover all of his lost territories and ruled against recognizing his seizure of the Baltic states and half of Poland. Our fear of another uproar in this country over "secret treaties," such as had been raised after World War I, and of the outcry of Polish and other citizens, combined with aversion to any extension of the area of communism to prevent the British from making a more realistic agreement with Russia in April 1942.

Then the British managed to lead Western war operations through peripheral warfare in North Africa, Sicily, and Italy until May 1944. This was justifiable strategy for us, but it left the main brunt of the land war on the Russians to the end and created in their minds lasting suspicions of being deliberately sacrificed. More important, it gave the Russian armies time to come into Central Europe, at the cost of many hundreds of thousands of casualties, losses which we would have suffered had we struck sooner and directly at Germany.

All during the war years Churchill sought manfully to retrieve in East Europe what Chamberlain had given away. His eyes were always on the non-existent "soft underbelly" of Europe, then in the late stages of the war on an invasion through Trieste, and finally for lunges into Germany to seize areas beyond the agreed zones of occupation for bargaining purposes. But always the actual balance of forces defeated him. The Russians were required to maul the bulk of the German forces to the last day of the war. Allied forces thrown through Trieste might well have enabled the Russians to skirt the Baltic Sea and appear on the English Channel. Furthermore, attempts to change the zones of occupation against the Russians would have been rejected by allied public opinion. Long afterward General Bedell Smith, one of General Eisenhower's most trusted generals, recorded his conviction that it "would have been quite impossible in the light of world public opinion in our own country," and his advice to Churchill at the time was "that I didn't think his own public opinion would permit it."

Soviet control of East Europe was the price we paid for the years of appeasement of Hitler, and it was not a high price. In Toynbee's judgment "the Nazis would have conquered the world," if we and the Soviets had not combined our efforts. They would eventually have crossed the narrow gap of the South Atlantic to Brazil and the rest of South America, where strong fifth columns could have been organized in more than one country. By our war alliance with the Soviets we prevented the unification of the world by the Nazis. That was a victory beyond price, but, says Toynbee, we "could not have put down Hitler without consequently producing the situation with which all of us now find ourselves confronted."

All this was fully evident during the war and it is still true. C. B. Marshall has reminded us that we do not have to guess what the Axis powers would have done had they won. They set it down plainly in their Tripartite Alliance on September 27, 1940—"a pattern for the conquest of the rest of the world and the beleaguerment of the United States." Why then did we have ten years of cold war over Russia's control of East Europe and over her desire to have a military base on the Turkish Straits?

EAST EUROPE DIVIDED BY CHURCHILL AND STALIN

Early in October 1944 Churchill sought to come to terms with the inevitable. Over the strong opposition of our State Department, but with Roosevelt's permission, he went to Moscow to make a temporary agreement for three months concerning the Balkans.

On October 9 he proposed to Stalin that Russia have 90 per cent predominance in Rumania, others 10 per cent, and 75 per cent predominance in Bulgaria, others 25 per cent. In Greece Britain would have 90 per cent predominance, and others 10 per cent. The "predominance" was to be divided 50–50 in Hungary and Yugoslavia. Nothing was said about this division of influence being temporary.

Stalin accepted this proposal without a word. He permitted a really free election in Hungary, which the old ruling classes duly won, and he did his best to force Tito to honor the bargain about Yugoslavia. Also he held his hand completely while Churchill promptly crushed the left forces in Greece, thereby sealing his agreement with Churchill and committing Roosevelt to it, before Yalta.

The communist revolution in Bulgaria was already in full cry when the Yalta conference met. The overthrow in the preceding December of the mighty ELAS movement in Greece by the British army and the Greek officer caste had suggested to the Russians that something very similar could occur in Bulgaria, where the Bulgarian army officers used the coup d'état "as a normal political instrument." "People's Court" trials began on December 24, 1944, and cut down the Bulgarian army officers as with a scythe until the end of February 1945.

On March 6 the Soviet Government imposed a communist-led government upon Rumania, deposing the Rumanian conservatives. It was "very hard to think of any constructive alternative," since free elections in Rumania under their control would have been "an invitation to Fascism here more than elsewhere."

The situation was worst in Rumania, where government was notoriously "so corrupt that it is a synonym for corrupt government," but there was no country in East Europe, with the exception of Greece, where the kind of free elections we wanted would not have been controlled by the old ruling classes. They had manipulated the elections for generations. No free election had ever been held. The Hungarian landlords had been ruthless rulers for a thousand years, and elsewhere the cliques which ruled for their own benefit had virtually all of the knowledge of political manipulations. The Hungarian and Rumanian ruling groups had also sent two million conscripted troops deep into Russia, behind Hitler's armies.

FREE ELECTIONS

In these circumstances the question arises, why did Stalin agree at Yalta to conduct "free elections" in Eastern Europe? Why we demanded them was clear. That is the American way of doing things, subject to the operations of political machines, and we wanted very much to prevent East Europe from being communized. No one at Yalta dreamed of denying that the region must cease to be a hostile *cordon sanitaire* against the Soviet Union and become "friendly" politically to the Soviet Union. No one could deny that, with the Red armies at that moment across Poland, within thirty miles of Berlin, and beyond Budapest sweeping up the Danube, while the Western allies were still in France, set back by the Ardennes offensive.

But could governments friendly to Russia be obtained in this region by "free elections" in which the ruling groups participated freely? It was inconceivable that these groups could be friendly to Russia, or that communist Russia could think of depending on them. That was as incredible as that we should freely arrange for a communist government in France or Italy. The Soviets also happened to believe that their system of government was as valid as ours, and that they could really depend only upon it to stop East Europe from being used as an invasion corridor into the Soviet Union.

If the Americans at Yalta committed a fault, it was not in "giving away" East Europe. That had been done at Munich long before. It was in trying to achieve the impossible under the formula of "free elections." Yet free elections were in their blood and they could do no other than to believe that this was a solution which all must accept. On his side, it is not likely that Stalin thought the formula would prevent him from purging the long dominant elements in East Europe, whose hostility to Red Russia needed no further demonstration. These elections might be managed and "people's democracies" set up which would be acceptable to the Americans. He knew that the decisive settlement for the area had been made in his gentleman's agreement with Churchill, on October 9, 1944, and that its execution was already far advanced on both sides.

He was loyally holding to his side of the bargain with Churchill and he could hardly have believed that the Yalta formulas would disrupt allied relations as soon as the war was over and lead to long years of bitter cold war.

TRUMAN'S REVERSAL
OF THE ROOSEVELT–HULL POLICY

It is possible that if Roosevelt had lived the same deadly quarrel would have developed, though it is far more likely that he already understood the deeper forces involved and the impossibility of frustrating them. What made a clash certain was the accession of Truman just at the close of the war. He intended to carry out Roosevelt's engagements, loyally and fully, and to exact from Stalin the same complete fulfilment, including free elections in East Europe. This theme runs through the first volume of his memoirs.

However his methods were poles apart from those of Roosevelt and Hull. All through 1944, his last year in office, Hull had conducted off-the-record conferences with groups of editors, clergymen, and members of Congress, to explain to them how far the Russians had come with us, how they had been "locked up and isolated for a quarter of a century," used to receiving violent epithets. It would "take time for them to get into step," but they would do it. He urged that "we must be patient and forbearing. We cannot settle questions with Russia by threats. We must use friendly methods."

No one was more opposed than Hull to Soviet control of East Europe, "interfering with her neighbors," but as he left office his policy rested on two bases: to show the Russians by example how a great power should act and to continue in constant friendly discussion with them. "Consult them on every point. Engage in no 'cussin matches' with them."

Nothing could have been further from President Truman's approach. He quickly read all the dispatches about friction with Russia over German surrenders, listened to everybody who wanted to get tough with the Russians, and when Molotov came by on April 23, 1945, to pay his respects to the new President, he received such a dressing down that he complained at the end of it that no one had ever talked like that to him before.

This was exactly eleven days after Roosevelt's death. It took Truman just that long to reverse the entire Roosevelt-Hull approach to Russia and to inaugurate an era of toughness and ever greater toughness in our dealings with her. Then on August 6, 1945, the Hiroshima explosion gave him the means to back insistence on free elections in East Europe and when the London Conference of September 1945 deadlocked over this issue he made up his mind at once to contain Russia. It was at this moment that Lippmann, noting that we had terminated lend-lease "abruptly and brutally" and had drifted into an arms race with the Soviet Union, warned: "Let no one deceive himself. We are drifting toward a catastrophe."

To the already deep fears of Russia for her own security, thrice justified since 1914, was added a new and dreadful fear of a fourth Western attack, backed by the atomic bomb. From the psychological point of view the policy of toughness was "the worst treatment" that could have been devised. "If a patient is suffering from genuine fear, you do not cure his fears and establish a rational relationship with him by making him more afraid. You endeavor to show him patiently and by your actions toward him that he has nothing to fear."

Exactly the opposite course was followed, with increasing momentum. In the following spring of 1946 Churchill issued at Fulton, Missouri, and in President Truman's applauding presence, his call for an overwhelming preponderance of power against Russia, hinting broadly at later forcible interventions in East Europe. Nevertheless, peace was made in Europe during the remainder of 1946. In three sessions of the Council of Foreign Ministers and a conference of 21 nations in Paris, peace treaties were hammered out in substantially the terms established by the various armistices. Really free elections had been held in Hungary and there were many signs of relaxation of tension as the year closed.

RESULTS OF THE TRUMAN DOCTRINE

However, in February the British turned the burden of supporting Greece over to us and Truman seized the occasion to proclaim the doctrine of containment, on March 12, 1947, which George F. Kennan spelled out fully in the July issue of *Foreign Affairs* as "long term, patient but firm and vigilant containment of Russian expansive tendencies." Otherwise the Kremlin would take its time about filling every "nook and cranny available to it in the basin of world power."

On its face this was the rashest policy ever enunciated by any American leader. For the first time in history the encirclement of a great power was openly proclaimed. This power, too, was in firm possession of the great heartland of Eurasia. It had already demonstrated that it could industrialize itself quickly and enough to defeat Hitler's armies. What it would do, after the Cold War was declared by Churchill and Truman, was easily predictable by any average man. The Soviet Union would put up a bold front to cover its frightening post-war weakness and work mightily to gain strength to hold what it had and then break the encirclement.

This was a difficult undertaking, for not only was the Soviet Union frightfully devastated, but Eastern Europe was in nearly as bad shape. However, what the Soviet peoples had done twice already they could do again under the lash of containment. After the two gruelling forced marches, before 1941 and after the German invasion, they undertook still a third and within eleven years from 1946 they had achieved first their A-bomb in 1949, then the H-bomb in 1953 and the first ICBM in 1957. In all other vital respects also they had gained that position of strength which was our announced goal after March 1950.

In the course of containment, "negotiation from strength" and liberation, we revivified fully the machinery of totalitarian rule in Russia. As William A. Williams has pointed out: "Appearing as a classic and literal verification of Marx's most apocalyptic prophecy, the policy of containment strengthened the hand of every die-hard Marxist and every extreme Russian nationalist among the Soviet leadership."

Containment also gave Stalin total power over the Soviet peoples. Williams continues: Armed with the language and actions of containment, which underwrote and extended his existing power, Stalin could and did drive the Soviet people to the brink of collapse and, no doubt, to the thought of open resistance. But the dynamic of revolt was always blocked, even among those who did have access to the levels of authority, by the fact of containment and the open threat of liberation. Thus protected by his avowed enemies, Stalin was able to force his nation through extreme deprivations and extensive purges to the verge of physical and psychological exhaustion. But he also steered it through the perils of reconstruction to the security of nuclear parity with the United States."

Stalin's first reply to containment was the destruction of the Small-holder's Party in Hungary, between March and August 1947, into which he had allowed the dispossessed landlords to go, and to take over the Hungarian government in its first free elections. The ending of this government was not difficult, since a topnotch American newsman found in Hungary that the "political sterility" of these elements was so great and their inclinations toward corruption so "incorrigible" that an astonishing number of anti-communists accepted the communist claim to represent the people. The kind of democracy for which we had fought throughout East Europe might have been destroyed in Hungary anyway, but the Truman Doctrine made it a matter of life and death for the Hungarian Reds to end it.

FROM THE MARSHALL PLAN TO TOTAL DIPLOMACY

THE MARSHALL PLAN

Meanwhile the yawning economic void in West Europe had led to the American Marshall Plan, and offer of economic help to all the nations of Europe, a "policy not directed against any country or doctrine, but against hunger, poverty, desperation and chaos."

If this magnificent conception had come earlier, while the Russians were asking in vain for a six billion dollar loan, before UNRRA was abolished and before the Truman Doctrine had drawn the lines of conflict tightly, there would have been no Cold War. In the context of the declared Cold War, Russia not only rejected the Marshall Plan for herself but forbade her East European satellites to participate, foreseeing that the American largesse would dissolve shaky loyalties to her satellite governments in more than one East European quarter.

Molotov's angry departure from the Marshall Plan conference in Paris, on August 2, 1947, convinced much of Western opinion that Russia was hostile to the West and that she had deliberately split the world in two. Three months later Russia created the Cominform, an organization of all the Communist parties in East Europe, plus those of France and Italy, to back the Molotov Plan for East European reconstruction, to oppose the Marshall Plan and to fight the Cold War generally. This response to the Truman Doctrine and the Marshall Plan convinced many people throughout the West that the Russians had reverted to the world revolution and were plotting to take over the earth.

Then the Communist seizure of Czechoslovakia hardened this fear into frightened certainty. This high peak of the Cold War, in late February 1948, had been preceded by the announcement on January 22 of a plan for a Western Union in Europe, which the London *Times* later thought might have "provoked the Soviet Union to hurry forward its own plans" for the consolidation of the Communist bloc.

CZECHOSLOVAKIA

But Czechoslovakia had been lost to the West at Munich, and in the successive events of the German occupation, which had destroyed most of the conservative classes and made it impossible for the Czechs to wish to oppose Russia. Both the Truman Doctrine and the Marshall Plan had also made it certain that Russia would bring Czechoslovakia behind the Iron Curtain before long. When this happened, the West lost nothing from the power standpoint. On broader grounds it was a time for sorrow and remorse that big power politics had twice deprived the Czechs of the democracy and freedom they did not deserve to lose either time.

However, all this was forgotten in the wave of shock, alarm and anger which swept over the West. Within a month the five power Western Union treaty was signed and on the same day, March 25, 1948, President Truman made an address in which he developed the devil theory fully. One nation, and one alone, had refused to cooperate in making peace, had broken the agreements it did make, had obstructed the United Nations and destroyed both the independence and the democratic character of a whole series of nations in Central and East Europe. To stop this nation Truman demanded prompt passage of ERP, more funds for Greece, Turkey and Chiang Kai-shek, and universal military training.

Thereafter the United States proceeded rapidly along an essentially negative course, in which we rushed to counter each communist move, tied up our resources in blocking efforts, selected our friends on one test alone, and rapidly adopted at home the methods and weapons of "the enemy."

BERLIN BLOCKADE

There is more cause for satisfaction in our handling of the Berlin blockade from June 1948 to May 1949. The Russians had a strong case for terminating the four power occupation of Berlin, because the West had announced plans on June 7 for the creation of a West German government. Since the four power occupation of Berlin was based on the assumption that Berlin would be the capital of a united Germany, the quadripartite occupation did become an anomaly when the assumption was destroyed. Thereafter West Berlin became from the Russian standpoint only a listening post and spy center for the West in the center of East Germany, and an ideological thorn in her side.

The announcement of a new currency for West Germany, imperatively needed, also created urgent problems for East Germany, since it would circulate in Berlin.

These were real grievances, but from the Western standpoint they did not justify an attempt to starve out 2,000,000 West Berliners. The crisis was grave and it was met by the West imaginatively, boldly and resolutely. The advocates of sending an army of tanks to Berlin were silenced and the air-lift did the job, dramatically lifting allied prestige to new heights. In this engagement of the Cold War the action of the West was a model of combined courage and restraint, and President Truman deserves his large share of the credit for it.

"TOTAL DIPLOMACY"

The Cold War as proclaimed by Churchill and Truman would have been impractical from the start had it not been for the American A-bomb monopoly, in which both leaders took the deepest satisfaction. When it was abruptly ended in September 1949, long before the expected time, a severe crisis of confidence shook Washington, a crisis which was ended by the decision to produce H-bombs and rearm further for the successful prosecution of the Cold War. It would be a long pull and take very steady nerves, Secretary of State Acheson explained on three occasions early in 1950, but the Russian river of aggression would be contained.

Restored confidence was expressed in Acheson's Berkeley speech of March 16, 1950, in which he laid down seven pre-conditions for negotiation with Russia amounting to Soviet surrender of its positions before negotiation.

KOREA

Then on June 25, 1950, the Russian river of aggression actually moved into Western held territory for the first time when the North Koreans invaded South Korea. Hardly anyone in the West questioned this verdict. Yet there were two other equally strong probabilities: that the North Koreans plunged southward on their own initiative, and that Syngman Rhee provoked them to do so by taking the initiative along the border in the day or two after the UN observers returned to Seoul. That he would be wholly capable of precipitating a war for the unification of Korea has been amply demonstrated several times since. Both sides in Korea were highly keyed for civil war, each intent on unification its way.

Ingram's conclusion is sound when he says: "Nor are we in possession of any positive proof that in Korea or elsewhere she (Russia) has conspired to instigate minor war against the Western allies through one of her satellites." He adds that "suspicions are not proof" and doubts that any evidence can be found later to sustain the charge that the Korean trouble arose as the result of a plot by China, or the Soviet Union, or both, to embarrass the West.

No doubts on this score entered the minds of our leaders in June 1950. It was assumed at once that the Kremlin had ordered the invasion and that this was the first of a series of satellite wars which would stampede both Asia and eventually West Europe into the Soviet camp, unless this attempt were promptly scotched. The United Nations was instantly mobilized, to minimize the shock of our intervention in an Asiatic civil war.

If our cold war purpose had not been predominant, the defeat of the North Korean aggression would have been a great victory for collective security and the United Nations. As the crisis did develop the UN Security Council approved our military action before it had heard the North Koreans, and it never did hear them—a serious breach of normal, fair procedure.

Then when the 38th Parallel was recovered, within three months and relatively painlessly, the monumental error was committed of trying to abolish the North Korean state. This mistake ranks close behind our failure to lead the League of Nations and our enunciation of the Truman Doctrine among the foreign policy errors committed by the United States. It was a political mistake of the first magnitude because it challenged both China and Russia in the North Korean triangle, a strategic area of the utmost importance to them. Moreover, it challenged them as communist powers to permit the Americans to destroy a communist state in their own front yards and set up a model capitalist democracy. It was a military gamble because it launched our armies precipitately into untenable territory. It was a moral blunder because it invalidated the central idea of the United Nations that it is a police force and not a partisan belligerent. When the United Nations invaded North Korea "they were no longer acting as police, but as co-belligerents on the side of the South Koreans."

Consequently, when China intervened on behalf of the North Koreans "the United Nations by becoming belligerents instead of a police force were no longer morally entitled to indict China." But she was indicted as an aggressor, under total pressure from Washington, and is still excluded from the United Nations on that ground.

Thus what should have been a brief, successful UN police operation was converted into a full-scale war which dragged on for three more years, always on the edge of a world war, until neutralism had been made a world movement, until the whole idea of the United Nations being a policeman had been made highly doubtful, and until President Truman and his party had been driven from office, more because of "Truman's war," never declared by Congress, than for any other reason. The war had become to the American people a never ending horror in a far country, for veiled cold war reasons.

TRUMAN'S LEADERSHIP

The tragedy of the second war in Korea brought out sharply both the defects and the good qualities of President Truman's leadership. His ability to make up his mind and act is a great quality in a ruler. Without it he is lost. But it is not the only quality necessary. There are occasions, perhaps more of them, when restraint is what is needed. There are even times when a President must have "the courage to be timid" or to seem so. Restraint is a far greater virtue than rashness. Truman could plunge in easily and too far, but he did not expand the second Korean war into World War III, as so many urged him to do, and he finally recalled General MacArthur who had flagrantly exceeded his instructions and was leading the cry for a greater war. Thus Truman did not compound his great Korean error into an irretrievable one, even when there was a widespread, angry belief that the Kremlin planned to bleed us white in a series of satellite wars around Russia's vast perimeter— accepting the challenge and logic of the Truman Doctrine.

On the great issue of the Chinese Revolution Truman also avoided disaster. His Doctrine was breached in gigantic fashion by the Communist Revolution in China, and his political enemies pushed him relentlessly to enforce it there, but he had the good sense to send his greatest lieutenant, General Marshall, to China for a long effort to mediate the Chinese civil war, and afterwards he accepted Marshall's report that we could not settle that gigantic conflict. It must have been difficult to put his Doctrine into abeyance, in the place where it was violated on the greatest scale, but he did it and avoided inaugurating a third world war by that route.

By 1950, an experienced editor and biographer could write of Truman: "In 1945 the moral hegemony of the world was within his grasp, but it has slipped from his fingers."

At the close of his presidency the moral leadership of the world had passed in large part to Nehru, the neutral opponent of the Cold War, but much of it went begging for lack of a truly powerful voice. Truman, who might have voiced it, had become only the belligerent leader of an anti-Soviet, anti-communist crusade.

2 The Development of the Cold War

Not long after the Yalta conference it became clear that the allies disagreed on the interpretation of its terms. The Russians had promised self-determination and free elections in Eastern Europe. It soon became apparent that by Western standards these promises were not being kept. In the following letter written shortly before his death Roosevelt complains to Stalin.

President Roosevelt's Letter to Marshal Stalin

Received on April 1, 1945

Personal and Top Secret for Marshal Stalin
from President Roosevelt

I CANNOT CONCEAL FROM YOU the concern with which I view the developments of events of mutual interest since our fruitful meeting at Yalta. The decisions we reached there were good ones and have for the most part been welcomed with enthusiasm by the peoples of the world who saw in our ability to find a common basis of understanding the best pledge for a secure and peaceful world after this war. Precisely because of the hopes and expectations that these decisions raised, their fulfillment is being followed with the closest attention. We have no right to let them be disappointed. So far there has been a discouraging lack of progress made in the carrying out, which the world expects, of the political decisions which we reached at the conference particularly those relating to the Polish question. I am frankly puzzled as to why this should be and must tell you that I do not fully understand in many respects the apparent indifferent attitude of your Gov-

Ministry of Foreign Affairs of the U.S.S.R., *Correspondence Between the Chairman of the Council of Ministers of the U.S.S.R. and the Presidents of the U.S.A. and the Prime Ministers of Great Britain During the Great Patriotic War of 1941–1945*, II (1957), 201–4.

ernment. Having understood each other so well at Yalta I am convinced that the three of us can and will clear away any obstacles which have developed since then. I intend, therefore, in this message to lay before you with complete frankness the problem as I see it.

Although I have in mind primarily the difficulties which the Polish negotiations have encountered, I must make a brief mention of our agreement embodied in the Declaration on Liberated Europe. I frankly cannot understand why the recent developments in Roumania should be regarded as not falling within the terms of that Agreement. I hope you will find time personally to examine the correspondence between our Governments on this subject.

However, the part of our agreements at Yalta which has aroused the greatest popular interest and is the most urgent relates to the Polish question. You are aware of course that the Commission which we set up has made no progress. I feel this is due to the interpretation which your Government is placing upon the Crimea decisions. In order that there shall be no misunderstanding I set forth below my interpretations of the points of the Agreement which are pertinent to the difficulties encountered by the Commission in Moscow.

In the discussions that have taken place so far your Government appears to take the position that the new Polish Provisional Government of National Unity which we agreed should be formed should be little more than a continuation of the present Warsaw Government. I cannot reconcile this either with our agreement or our discussions. While it is true that the Lublin Government is to be reorganized and its members play a prominent role, it is to be done in such a fashion as to bring into being a new government. This point is clearly brought out in several places in the text of the Agreement. I must make it quite plain to you that any such solution which would result in a thinly disguised continuance of the present Warsaw régime would be unacceptable and would cause the people of the United States to regard the Yalta agreement as having failed.

It is equally apparent that for the same reason the Warsaw Government cannot under the Agreement claim the right to select or reject what Poles are to be brought to Moscow by the Commission for consultation. Can we not agree that it is up to the Commission to select the Polish leaders to come to Moscow to consult in the first instance and invitations be sent out accordingly. If this could be done I see no great objection to having the Lublin group come first in order that they may be fully acquainted with the agreed interpretation of the Yalta decisions on this point. It is of course understood that if the Lublin group come first no arrangements would be made independently with them before the arrival of the other Polish leaders called for consultation. In order to facilitate the agreement the Commission might first of all select a small but representative group of Polish leaders who could suggest other names for the consideration of the Commission. We have not and would not bar or veto any candidate for consultation which Mr. Molotov might propose, being confident that he would not suggest any Poles who would be inimical to the intent of the Crimea decision. I feel that it is not too much to ask that my Ambassador be accorded the same confidence and that any candidate for consultation presented by any one of the Commission be accepted by the others in good faith. It is obvious to me that if the right of the Commission to select these Poles is limited or shared with the Warsaw Government the very foundation on which our agreement rests would be destroyed.

While the foregoing are the immediate obstacles which in my opinion have prevented our Commission from making any progress in this vital matter, there are two other suggestions which were not in the agreement but nevertheless have a very important bearing on the result we all seek. Neither of these suggestions has been as yet accepted by your Government. I refer to:

(1) That there should be the maximum of political tranquility in Poland and that dissident groups should cease any measures and counter-measures against each other. That we should respectively use our influence to that end seems to me eminently reasonable.

(2) It would also seem entirely natural in view of the responsibilities placed upon them by the Agreement that representatives of the American and British members of the Commission should be permitted to visit Poland. As you will recall Mr. Molotov himself suggested this at an early meeting of the Commission and only subsequently withdrew it.

I wish I could convey to you how important it is for the successful development of our program of international collaboration that this Polish question be settled fairly and speedily. If this is not done all of the difficulties and dangers to Allied unity which we had so much in mind in reaching our decisions at the Crimea will face us in an even more acute form. You are, I am sure, aware that the genuine popular support in the United States is required to carry out any government policy, foreign or domestic. The American people make up their own mind and no government action can change it. I mention this fact because the last sentence of your message about Mr. Molotov's attendance at San Francisco made me wonder whether you give full weight to this factor.

One of the Russian grievances was America's cessation of lend-lease shipments after the end of the European War. In the following selection, Secretary of State Byrnes reports Stalin's complaint and the American response.

F R O M *Speaking Frankly* BY JAMES F. BYRNES

H E [*Stalin—D. K.*] W A S P A R T I C U L A R L Y I R R I T A T E D by the manner in which lend-lease shipments had been suspended at the end of the European war. The fact that ships with supplies bound for Russia even had been unloaded indicated to him that the cancellation order was an effort to put pressure on the Soviet Union. This, he declared, was a fundamental mistake and the United States should understand much could be gained from the Russians only if they were approached on a friendly basis.

In the case of the German Navy and merchant fleet, he had sent a message to the President and the Prime Minister suggesting that one-third be turned over to the Soviets. Not only had he received no reply, he said, but he had acquired instead an impression that the request was to be rejected.

These complaints were surprising to us at home. They revealed an extreme sensitivity and an amazing degree of almost instinctive suspicion.

Mr. Hopkins forcefully and tactfully presented the position of the United States. As for the German ships, it was our intention that they should be divided equally among the three and we thought that the matter could be settled at the forthcoming meeting of the Big Three. He explained that the cancellation of lend-lease was necessary under the law because lend-lease was authorized only for the purpose of prosecuting the war. With the German war ended and with the Soviet Union not yet a participant in the Japanese war, further shipment could not be justified. The order to unload the ships was the mistake of an official who had nothing to do with policy, and the order had been withdrawn quickly. He reminded the Marshal of how liberally the United States had construed the law in sending foodstuffs and other nonmilitary items to their aid.

Stalin readily acknowledged the accuracy of Hopkins' statement. If proper warning had been given there would have been no feeling about the matter, he said, pointing out that advance notice was important to them because their economy is based on plans. The way in which the shipments had been halted made it impossible for him to express, as he had intended, the great appreciation of the Soviets for the lend-lease aid given to them.

James F. Byrnes, *Speaking Frankly* (1947), pp. 62–3. Reprinted by permission of James F. Byrnes Foundation.

Hopkins told the Marshal that what disturbed him most was the revelation that Stalin believed the United States would use lend-lease as a pressure weapon. The United States, he asserted, is a strong nation and does not need to indulge in such methods. With this, Stalin said he was fully satisfied with our explanation.

It is sometimes alleged that America's use of the atomic bomb to end the war in Asia was politically motivated and is evidence of American suspicion and hostility toward Russia even during the war. In the following selection, Norman Cousins and Thomas Finletter argue for such an interpretation.

FROM *A Beginning for Sanity*

BY NORMAN COUSINS AND THOMAS K. FINLETTER

SUMMING UP, the scientists expressed their conviction that a unilateral approach to the dropping of the bomb, even apart from moral considerations, however overwhelming, would almost inevitably result in unilateral action by other nations. And unilateralism in an atomic age was not merely a problem but a fatal disease. We would be undermining a possible common ground upon which common controls might later be built. As a corollary, we would be destroying whatever stand we might later decide to take on outlawing the use of atomic weapons in warfare. It would be naive to expect other nations to take such a plea seriously in view of our own lack of reticence in dropping the bomb when the war was on the very verge of being won without it.

Why, then, did we drop it? Or, assuming that the use of the bomb was justified, why did we not demonstrate its power in a test under the auspices of the UN, on the basis of which an ultimatum would be issued to Japan—transferring the burden of responsibility to the Japanese themselves?

In speculating upon possible answers to these questions, some facts available since the bombing may be helpful. We now know, for example, that Russia was scheduled to come into the war against Japan by August 8, 1945. Russia had agreed at Yalta to join the fight against Japan ninety days

Norman Cousins and Thomas K. Finletter, "A Beginning for Sanity," *The Saturday Review of Literature,* XXIV (June 15, 1946), 7–8. Reprinted by permission of *Saturday Review.*

after V-E day. Going after the knockout punch, we bombed Hiroshima on August 5, Nagasaki on August 7. Russia came into the war on August 8, as specified. Japan asked for surrender terms the same day.

Can it be that we were more anxious to prevent Russia from establishing a claim for full participation in the occupation against Japan than we were to think through the implications of unleashing atomic warfare? Whatever the answer, one thing seems likely: There was not enough time between July 16, when we knew at New Mexico that the bomb would work, and August 8, the Russian deadline date, for us to have set up the very complicated machinery of a test atomic bombing involving time-consuming problems of area preparations; invitations and arrangements for observers (the probability being that the transportation to the South Pacific would in itself exceed the time limit); issuance of an ultimatum and the conditions of fulfillment, even if a reply limit was set at only forty-eight hours or less—just to mention a few.

No; any test would have been impossible if the purpose was to knock Japan out before Russia came in—or at least before Russia could make anything other than a token of participation prior to a Japanese collapse.

It may be argued that this decision was justified, that it was a legitimate exercise of power politics in a rough-and-tumble world, that we thereby avoided a struggle for authority in Japan similar to what we have experienced in Germany and Italy, that unless we came out of the war with a decisive balance of power over Russia, we would be in no position to checkmate Russian expansion.

There is a dangerous plausibility here—a plausibility as inseparable from the war system of sovereign nations as armaments are from armaments races. It is the plausibility of power politics, of action leading to reaction, reaction leading to counter-reaction, and counter-reaction leading to war; of competitive systems of security rather than of workable world organization. It is a plausibility that rests on the flat assumption that war with Russia is inevitable, and that we should fight it at a time and under terms advantageous to us.

Such "plausibilities" are rejected by those who feel that the big job is to avert the next war, rather than to win it—even assuming that the next war will be worth winning, a somewhat dubious proposition. And they see no way to avert the next war other than through a world organization having the power to back up its decisions by law and relying upon preponderant force as needed. Such an organization would attempt to dispose of the fear-begetting-fear, provocation-begetting-provocation cycle; and to substitute in its place a central authority from which no member could withdraw or secede under any circumstances. It would automatically deprive potential aggressors of their traditional excuse for aggression—namely, their own encirclement and insecurity—and be strong enough to deal with them should a real threat arise.

The following selection shows the confusion and contradictions in the American government over Russian participation in the Asiatic war.

FROM *The Forrestal Diaries*

TALKED WITH BYRNES [now at Potsdam as American Secretary of State, having succeeded Mr. Stettinius on the conclusion of the San Francisco Conference]. . . . Byrnes said he was most anxious to get the Japanese affair over with before the Russians got in, with particular reference to Dairen and Port Arthur. Once in there, he felt, it would not be easy to get them out. . . .

Evidently on the question of Russian entry into the Pacific war the wheel was now coming full circle. Forrestal was to get a further side-light on this two years later at a reminiscent luncheon gathering at which General Dwight D. Eisenhower was present. "When President Truman came to Potsdam in the summer of 1945," Forrestal noted, "he told Eisenhower he had as one of his primary objectives that of getting Russia into the Japanese war. Eisenhower begged him at that time not to assume that he had to give anything away to do this, that the Russians were desperately anxious to get into the Eastern war and that in Eisenhower's opinion there was no question but that Japan was already thoroughly beaten. When the President told him at the end of the Conference that he had achieved his objectives and was going home, Eisenhower again remarked that he earnestly hoped the President had not had to make any concessions to get them in."

Still later Forrestal recorded his own conclusion. In a note of June 23, 1947, he observed that the Russians would have to come into the Marshall Plan; "they could no more afford to be out of it than they could have afforded not to join in the war against Japan (fifty divisions could not have kept them *out* of this war)." While Forrestal was mistaken about Soviet participation in the Marshall Plan, it does not follow that his estimate as to the Pacific war was wrong.

Next day, a Sunday, Forrestal wandered through the ruins of Berlin and was as deeply impressed by that staggering scene of destruction as are all who have seen it. He also found that others did not share what would seem to have been the President's rather optimistic mood about the Russians.

Walter Millis, ed., with the collaboration of E. S. Duffield, *The Forrestal Diaries* (1951), pp. 78–9. Reprinted by permission of Princeton University.

In 1946, the United States, which had a monopoly on the production of atomic weapons, offered to share its knowledge and submit to United Nations control of atomic energy. The Baruch plan, which is described in the following selection, was rejected by the Soviet Union.

FROM *United States Proposals for the International Control of Atomic Energy*

STATEMENT BY BERNARD M. BARUCH, UNITED STATES REPRESENTATIVE TO THE ATOMIC ENERGY COMMISSION, JUNE 14, 1946

My Fellow Members of the United Nations Atomic Energy Commission, and My Fellow Citizens of the World:

WE ARE HERE to make a choice between the quick and the dead.

That is our business.

Behind the black portent of the new atomic age lies a hope which, seized upon with faith, can work our salvation. If we fail, then we have damned every man to be the slave of Fear. Let us not deceive ourselves: We must elect World Peace or World Destruction.

Science has torn from nature a secret so vast in its potentialities that our minds cower from the terror it creates. Yet terror is not enough to inhibit the use of the atomic bomb. The terror created by weapons has never stopped man from employing them. For each new weapon a defense has been produced, in time. But now we face a condition in which adequate defense does not exist.

Science, which gave us this dread power, shows that it *can* be made a giant help to humanity, but science does *not* show us how to prevent its baleful use. So we have been appointed to obviate that peril by finding a meeting of the minds and the hearts of our peoples. Only in the will of mankind lies the answer.

It is to express this will and make it effective that we have been assembled. We must provide the mechanism to assure that atomic energy is used for peaceful purposes and preclude its use in war. To that end, we must provide immediate, swift, and sure punishment of those who violate the agreements that are reached by the nations. Penalization is essential if peace

Senate Committee on Foreign Relations, *A Decade of American Foreign Policy: Basic Documents, 1941–1949* (1950), pp. 1079–81, 1082–7.

is to be more than a feverish interlude between wars. And, too, the United Nations can prescribe individual responsibility and punishment on the principles applied at Nürnberg by the Union of Soviet Socialist Republics, The United Kingdom, France, and the United States—a formula certain to benefit the world's future.

In this crisis, we represent not only our governments but, in a larger way, we represent the peoples of the world. We must remember that the peoples do not belong to the governments but that the governments belong to the peoples. We must answer their demands; we must answer the world's longing for peace and security.

In that desire the United States shares ardently and hopefully. The search of science for the absolute weapon has reached fruition in this country. But she stands ready to proscribe and destroy this instrument—to lift its use from death to life—if the world will join in a pact to that end.

In our success lies the promise of a new life, freed from the heart-stopping fears that now beset the world. The beginning of victory for the great ideals for which millions have bled and died lies in building a workable plan. Now we approach fulfilment of the aspirations of mankind. At the end of the road lies the fairer, better, surer life we crave and mean to have.

Only by a lasting peace are liberties and democracies strengthened and deepened. War is their enemy. And it will not do to believe that any of us can escape war's devastation. Victor, vanquished, and neutrals alike are affected physically, economically, and morally.

Against the degradation of war we can erect a safeguard. That is the guerdon for which we reach. Within the scope of the formula we outline here there will be found, to those who seek it, the essential elements of our purpose. Others will see only emptiness. Each of us carries his own mirror in which is reflected hope—or determined desperation—courage or cowardice.

There is a famine throughout the world today. It starves men's bodies. But there is a greater famine—the hunger of men's spirit. That starvation can be cured by the conquest of fear, and the substitution of hope, from which springs faith—faith in each other; faith that we want to work together toward salvation; and determination that those who threaten the peace and safety shall be punished.

The peoples of these democracies gathered here have a particular concern with our answer, for their peoples hate war. They will have a heavy exaction to make of those who fail to provide an escape. They are not afraid of an internationalism that protects; they are unwilling to be fobbed off by mouthings about narrow sovereignty, which is today's phrase for yesterday's isolation.

The basis of a sound foreign policy, in this new age, for all the nations here gathered, is that: anything that happens, no matter where or how, which menaces the peace of the world, or the economic stability concerns each and all of us.

That, roughly, may be said to be the central theme of the United Nations. It is with that thought we begin consideration of the most important subject that can engage mankind—life itself.

The United States proposes the creation of an International Atomic Development Authority, to which should be entrusted all phases of the development and use of atomic energy, starting with the raw material and including—

1. Managerial control or ownership of all atomic-energy activities potentially dangerous to world security.
2. Power to control, inspect, and license all other atomic activities.
3. The duty of fostering the beneficial uses of atomic energy.
4. Research and development responsibilities of an affirmative character intended to put the Authority in the forefront of atomic knowledge and thus to enable it to comprehend, and therefore to detect, misuse of atomic energy. To be effective the Authority must itself be the world's leader in the field of atomic knowledge and development and thus supplement its legal authority with the great power inherent in possession of leadership in knowledge.

I offer this as a basis for beginning our discussion.

But I think the peoples we serve would not believe—and without faith nothing counts—that a treaty, merely outlawing possession or use of the atomic bomb, constitutes effective fulfilment of the instructions to this Commission. Previous failures have been recorded in trying the method of simple renunciation, unsupported by effective guaranties of security and armament limitation. No one would have faith in that approach alone.

Now, if ever, is the time to act for the common good. Public opinion supports a world movement toward security. If I read the signs aright, the peoples want a program not composed merely of pious thoughts but of enforceable sanctions—an international law with teeth in it.

We of this nation, desirous of helping to bring peace to the world and realizing the heavy obligations upon us arising from our possession of the means of producing the bomb and from the fact that it is part of our armament, are prepared to make our full contribution toward effective control of atomic energy.

When an adequate system for control of atomic energy, including the renunciation of the bomb as a weapon, has been agreed upon and put into effective operation and condign punishments set up for violations of the rules of control which are to be stigmatized as international crimes, we propose that—

1. Manufacture of atomic bombs shall stop;
2. Existing bombs shall be disposed of pursuant to the terms of the treaty, and
3. The Authority shall be in possession of full information as to the know-how for the production of atomic energy.

Let me repeat, so as to avoid misunderstanding: my country is ready to make its full contribution toward the end we seek, subject of course, to our constitutional processes, and to an adequate system of control becoming fully effective, as we finally work it out.

Now as to violations: in the agreement, penalties of as serious a nature as the nations may wish and as immediate and certain in their execution as possible, should be fixed for:

1. Illegal possession or use of an atomic bomb;
2. Illegal possession, or separation, of atomic material suitable for use in an atomic bomb;
3. Seizure of any plant or other property belonging to or licensed by the Authority;
4. Wilful interference with the activities of the Authority;
5. Creation or operation of dangerous projects in a manner contrary to, or in the absence of, a license granted by the international control body.

It would be a deception, to which I am unwilling to lend myself, were I not to say to you and to our peoples, that the matter of punishment lies at the very heart of our present security system. It might as well be admitted, here and now, that the subject goes straight to the veto power contained in the Charter of the United Nations so far as it relates to the field of atomic energy. The Charter permits penalization only by concurrence of each of the five great powers—Union of Soviet Socialist Republics, the United Kingdom, China, France and the United States.

I want to make very plain that I am concerned here with the veto power only as it affects this particular problem. There must be no veto to protect those who violate their solemn agreements not to develop or use atomic energy for destructive purposes.

The bomb does not wait upon debate. To delay may be to die. The time between violation and preventive action or punishment would be all too short for extended discussion as to the course to be followed.

As matters now stand several years may be necessary for another country to produce a bomb, *de novo*. However, once the basic information is generally known, and the Authority has established producing plants for peaceful purposes in the several countries, an illegal seizure of such a plant might permit a malevolent nation to produce a bomb in 12 months, and if preceded by secret preparation and necessary facilities perhaps even in a much shorter time. The time required—the advance warning given of the possible use of a bomb—can only be generally estimated but obviously will depend upon many factors, including the success with which the Authority has been able to introduce elements of safety in the design of its plants and the degree to which illegal and secret preparation for the military use of atomic energy will have been eliminated. Presumably no nation would think of starting a war with only one bomb.

This shows how imperative speed is in detecting and penalizing violations.

The process of prevention and penalization—a problem of profound statecraft—is, as I read it, implicit in the Moscow statement, signed by the Union of Soviet Socialist Republics, the United States, and the United Kingdom a few months ago.

But before a country is ready to relinquish any winning weapons it must have more than words to reassure it. It must have a guarantee of safety, not only against the offenders in the atomic area but against the illegal users of other weapons—bacteriological, biological, gas—perhaps—why not?—against the war itself.

In the elimination of war lies our solution, for only then will nations cease to compete with one another in the production and use of dread "secret" weapons which are evaluated solely by their capacity to kill. This devilish program takes us back not merely to the Dark Ages, but from cosmos to chaos. If we succeed in finding a suitable way to control atomic weapons, it is reasonable to hope that we may also preclude the use of other weapons adaptable to mass destruction. When a man learns to say "A" he can, if he chooses, learn the rest of the alphabet, too.

Let this be anchored in our minds:

Peace is never long preserved by weight of metal or by an armament race. Peace can be made tranquil and secure only by understanding and agreement fortified by sanctions. We must embrace international cooperation or international disintegration.

Science has taught us how to put the atom to work. But to make it work for good instead of for evil lies in the domain dealing with the principles of human duty. We are now facing a problem more of ethics than of physics.

The solution will require apparent sacrifice in pride and in position, but better pain as the price of peace than death as the price of war.

I now submit the following measures as representing the fundamental features of a plan which would give effect to certain of the conclusions which I have epitomized.

1. *General.* The Authority should set up a thorough plan for control of the field of atomic energy, through various forms of ownership, dominion, licenses, operation, inspection, research and management by competent personnel. After this is provided for, there should be as little interference as may be with the economic plans and the present private, corporate and state relationships in the several countries involved.

2. *Raw Materials.* The Authority should have as one of its earliest purposes to obtain and maintain complete and accurate information on world supplies of uranium and thorium and to bring them under its dominion. The precise pattern of control for various types of deposits of such materials will have to depend upon the geological, mining, refining, and economic facts involved in different situations.

The Authority should conduct continuous surveys so that it will have the most complete knowledge of the world geology of uranium and thorium. Only after all current information on world sources of uranium and thorium is known to us all can equitable plans be made for their production, refining, and distribution.

3. *Primary Production Plants.* The Authority should exercise complete managerial control of the production of fissionable materials. This means that it should control and operate all plants producing fissionable materials in dangerous quantities and must own and control the product of these plants.

4. *Atomic Explosives.* The Authority should be given sole and exclusive right to conduct research in the field of atomic explosives. Research activities in the field of atomic explosives are essential in order that the Authority may keep in the forefront of knowledge in the field of atomic energy and fulfil the objective of preventing illicit manufacture of bombs. Only by maintaining its position as the best-informed agency will the Authority be able to determine the line between intrinsically dangerous and non-dangerous activities.

5. *Strategic Distribution of Activities and Materials.* The activities entrusted exclusively to the Authority because they are intrinsically dangerous to security should be distributed throughout the world. Similarly, stockpiles of raw materials and fissionable materials should not be centralized.

6. *Non-Dangerous Activities.* A function of the Authority should be promotion of the peacetime benefits of atomic energy.

Atomic research (except in explosives), the use of research reactors, the production of radioactive tracers by means of non-dangerous reactors, the use of such tracers, and to some extent the production of power should be open to nations and their citizens under reasonable licensing arrangements from the Authority. Denatured materials, whose use we know also requires suitable safeguards, should be furnished for such purposes by the Authority under lease or other arrangement. Denaturing seems to have been overestimated by the public as a safety measure.

7. *Definition of Dangerous and Non-Dangerous Activities.* Although a reasonable dividing line can be drawn between dangerous and non-dangerous activities, it is not hard and fast. Provision should, therefore, be made to assure constant reexamination of the questions and to permit revision of the dividing line as changing conditions and new discoveries may require.

8. *Operations of Dangerous Activities.* Any plant dealing with uranium or thorium after it once reaches the potential of dangerous use must be not only subject to the most rigorous and competent inspection by the Authority, but its actual operation shall be under the management, supervision, and control of the Authority.

9. *Inspection.* By assigning intrinsically dangerous activities exclusively to

the Authority, the difficulties of inspection are reduced. If the Authority is the only agency which may lawfully conduct dangerous activities, then visible operation by others than the Authority will constitute an unambiguous danger signal. Inspection will also occur in connection with the licensing functions of the Authority.

10. *Freedom of Access.* Adequate ingress and egress for all qualified representatives of the Authority must be assured. Many of the inspection activities of the Authority should grow out of, and be incidental to, its other functions. Important measures of inspection will be associated with the tight control of raw materials, for this is a keystone of the plan. The continuing activities of prospecting, survey, and research in relation to raw materials will be designed not only to serve the affirmative development functions of the Authority, but also to assure that no surreptitious operations are conducted in the raw materials field by nations or their citizens.

11. *Personnel.* The personnel of the Authority should be recruited on a basis of proven competence but also so far as possible on an international basis.

12. *Progress by Stages.* A primary step in the creation of the system of control is the setting forth, in comprehensive terms, of the functions, responsibilities, powers and limitations of the Authority. Once a Charter for the Authority has been adopted, the Authority and the system of control for which it will be responsible will require time to become fully organized and effective. The plan of control will, therefore, have to come into effect in successive stages. These should be specifically fixed in the Charter or means should be otherwise set forth in the Charter for transitions from one stage to another, as contemplated in the resolution of the United Nations Assembly which created this Commission.

13. *Disclosures.* In the deliberations of the United Nations Commission on Atomic Energy, the United States is prepared to make available the information essential to a reasonable understanding of the proposals which it advocates. Further disclosures must be dependent, in the interests of all, upon the effective ratification of the treaty. When the Authority is actually created, the United States will join the other nations in making available the further information essential to that organization for the performance of its functions. As the successive stages of international control are reached, the United States will be prepared to yield, to the extent required by each stage, national control of activities in this field to the Authority.

14. *International Control.* There will be questions about the extent of control to be allowed to national bodies, when the Authority is established. Purely national authorities for control and development of atomic energy should to the extent necessary for the effective operation of the Authority be subordinate to it. This is neither an endorsement nor a disapproval of

the creation of national authorities. The Commission should evolve a clear demarcation of the scope of duties and responsibilities of such national authorities.

And now I end. I have submitted an outline for present discussion. Our consideration will be broadened by the criticism of the United States proposals and by the plans of the other nations, which, it is to be hoped, will be submitted at their early convenience. I and my associates of the United States Delegation will make available to each member of this body books and pamphlets, including the Acheson–Lilienthal report, recently made by the United States Department of State, and the McMahon Committee Monograph No. 1 entitled "Essential Information on Atomic Energy" relating to the McMahon Bill recently passed by the United States Senate, which may prove of value in assessing the situation.

All of us are consecrated to making an end of gloom and hopelessness. It will not be an easy job. The way is long and thorny, but supremely worth traveling. All of us want to stand erect, with our faces to the sun, instead of being forced to burrow into the earth, like rats.

The pattern of salvation must be worked out by all for all.

The light at the end of the tunnel is dim, but our path seems to grow brighter as we actually begin our journey. We cannot yet light the way to the end. However, we hope the suggestions of my government will be illuminating.

Let us keep in mind the exhortation of Abraham Lincoln, whose words, uttered at a moment of shattering national peril, form a complete text for our deliberation. I quote, paraphrasing slightly:

"We cannot escape history. We of this meeting will be remembered in spite of ourselves. No personal significance or insignificance can spare one or another of us. The fiery trial through which we are passing will light us down in honor or dishonor to the latest generation.

"We say we are for Peace. The world will not forget that we say this. We know how to save Peace. The world knows that we do. We, even we here, hold the power and have the responsibility.

"We shall nobly save, or meanly lose, the last, best hope of earth. The way is plain, peaceful, generous, just—a way which, if followed, the world will forever applaud."

My thanks for your attention.

*On March 5, 1946, Winston Churchill, in a speech at West-
minster College in Fulton, Missouri, gave public recognition to the division that had arisen between the former
allies.*

FROM *Winston Churchill's Speech at Fulton*

EUROPE DIVIDED

A SHADOW HAS FALLEN upon the scenes so lately lighted by the Allied
victory. Nobody knows what Soviet Russia and its Communist international
organization intends to do in the immediate future, or what are the limits, if
any, to their expansive and proselytizing tendencies. I have a strong admira-
tion and regard for the valiant Russian people and for my war-time comrade,
Marshal Stalin. There is sympathy and good will in Britain—and I doubt not
here also—toward the peoples of all the Russias and a resolve to persevere
through many differences and rebuffs in establishing lasting friendships. We
understand the Russians need to be secure on her western frontiers from all
renewal of German aggression. We welcome her to her rightful place among
the leading nations of the world. Above all we welcome constant, frequent
and growing contacts between the Russian people and our own people on
both sides of the Atlantic. It is my duty, however, to place before you certain
facts about the present position in Europe—I am sure I do not wish to, but it
is my duty, I feel, to present them to you.

From Stettin in the Baltic to Triest in the Adriatic, an iron curtain has
descended across the Continent. Behind that line lie all the capitals of the
ancient states of central and eastern Europe. Warsaw, Berlin, Prague,
Vienna, Budapest, Belgrade, Bucharest and Sofia, all these famous cities and
the populations around them lie in the Soviet sphere and all are subject in
one form or another, not only to Soviet influence but to a very high and
increasing measure of control from Moscow. Athens alone, with its immortal
glories, is free to decide its future at an election under British, American and
French observation. The Russian-dominated Polish government has been
encouraged to make enormous and wrongful inroads upon Germany, and
mass expulsions of millions of Germans on a scale grievous and undreamed
of are now taking place. The Communist parties, which were very small in
all these eastern states of Europe, have been raised to pre-eminence and
power far beyond their numbers and are seeking everywhere to obtain

Vital Speeches of the Day, XII (March 15, 1946), 331–2. Reprinted by permission of City News
Publishing Co.

totalitarian control. Police governments are prevailing in nearly every case, and so far, except in Czechoslovakia, there is no true democracy. Turkey and Persia are both profoundly alarmed and disturbed at the claims which are made upon them and at the pressure being exerted by the Moscow government. An attempt is being made by the Russians in Berlin to build up a quasi-Communist party in their zone of occupied Germany by showing special favors to groups of Left-Wing German leaders. At the end of the fighting last June, the American and British armies withdrew westward, in accordance with an earlier agreement, to a depth at some points 150 miles on a front of nearly 400 miles to allow the Russians to occupy this vast expanse of territory which the western democracies had conquered. If now the Soviet government tries, by separate action, to build up a pro-Communist Germany in their areas this will cause new serious difficulties in the British and American zones, and will give the defeated Germans the power of putting themselves up to auction between the Soviets and western democracies. Whatever conclusions may be drawn from these facts—and facts they are— this is certainly not the liberated Europe we fought to build up. Nor is it one which contains the essentials of permanent peace.

The safety of the world, ladies and gentlemen, requires a new unity in Europe from which no nation should be permanently outcast.

It is impossible not to comprehend—twice we have seen them drawn by irresistible forces in time to secure the victory but only after frightful slaughter and devastation have occurred. Twice the United States has had to send millions of its young men to fight a war, but now war can find any nation between dusk and dawn. Surely we should work within the structure of the United Nations and in accordance with our charter. That is an open course of policy.

COMMUNIST FIFTH COLUMNS

In front of the iron curtain which lies across Europe are other causes for anxiety. In Italy the Communist party is seriously hampered by having to support the Communist trained Marshal Tito's claims to former Italian territory at the head of the Adriatic. Nevertheless the future of Italy hangs in the balance. Again one cannot imagine a regenerated Europe without a strong France. All my public life I have worked for a strong France and I never lost faith in her destiny, even in the darkest hours. I will not lose faith now. However, in a great number of countries, far from the Russian frontiers and throughout the world, Communist fifth columns are established and work in complete unity and absolute obedience to the directions they receive from the Communist center. Except in the British Commonwealth and in this United States, where Communism is in its infancy, the Communist parties or fifth columns constitute a growing challenge and peril to Christian civilization. These are somber facts for any one to have to recite on the morrow of a victory gained by so much splendid comradeship in arms and in the cause of freedom and democracy, and we should be most unwise not to face them squarely while time remains.

The outlook is also anxious in the Far East and especially in Manchuria. The agreement which was made at Yalta, to which I was a party, was extremely favorable to Soviet Russia, but it was made at a time when no one could say that the German war might not extend all through the summer and autumn of 1945 and when the Japanese war was expected to last for a further eighteen months from the end of the German war. In this country you are all so well informed about the Far East, and such devoted friends of China, that I do not need to expatiate on the situation there.

I have felt bound to portray the shadow which, alike in the West and in the East, falls upon the world. I was a minister at the time of the Versailles treaty and a close friend of Mr. Lloyd George. I did not myself agree with many things that were done, but I have a very vague impression in my mind of that situation, and I find it painful to contrast it with that which prevails now. In those days there were high hopes and unbounded confidence that the wars were over, and that the League of Nations would become all-powerful. I do not see or feel the same confidence or even the same hopes in the haggard world at this time.

WAR NOT INEVITABLE

On the other hand I repulse the idea that a new war is inevitable; still more that it is imminent. It is because I am so sure that our fortunes are in our own hands and that we hold the power to save the future, that I feel the duty to speak out now that I have an occasion to do so. I do not believe that Soviet Russia desires war. What they desire is the fruits of war and the indefinite expansion of their power and doctrines. But what we have to consider here today while time remains, is the permanent prevention of war and the establishment of conditions of freedom and democracy as rapidly as possible in all countries. Our difficulties and dangers will not be removed by closing our eyes to them. They will not be removed by mere waiting to see what happens; nor will they be relieved by a policy of appeasement. What is needed is a settlement and the longer this is delayed the more difficult it will be and the greater our dangers will become. From what I have seen of our Russian friends and allies during the war, I am convinced that there is nothing they admire so much as strength, and there is nothing for which they have less respect than for military weakness. For that reason the old doctrine of a balance of power is unsound. We cannot afford, if we can help it, to work on narrow margins, offering temptations to a trial of strength. If the western democracies stand together in strict adherence to the principles of the United Nations Charter, their influence for furthering these principles will be immense and no one is likely to molest them. If, however, they become divided or falter in their duty, and if these all-important years are allowed to slip away, then indeed catastrophe may overwhelm us all.

Last time I saw it all coming, and cried aloud to my fellow countrymen and to the world, but no one paid any attention. Up till the year 1933 or even 1935, Germany might have been saved from the awful fate which has overtaken her and we might all have been spared the miseries Hitler let loose upon mankind. There never was a war in all history easier to prevent by timely action than the one which has just desolated such great areas of the globe. It could have been prevented without the firing of a single shot, and Germany might be powerful, prosperous and honored today, but no one would listen and one by one we were all sucked into the awful whirlpool. We surely must not let that happen again. This can only be achieved by reaching now, in 1946, a good understanding on all points with Russia under the general authority of the United Nations Organization and by the maintenance of that good understanding through many peaceful years, by the world instrument, supported by the whole strength of the English-speaking world and all its connections.

Let no man underrate the abiding power of the British Empire and Commonwealth. Because you see the forty-six millions in our island harassed about their food supply, of which they grew only one half, even in war time, or because we have difficulty in restarting our industries and export trade after six years of passionate war effort, do not suppose that we shall not come through these dark years of privation as we have come through the glorious years of agony, or that half a century from now you will not see seventy or eighty millions of Britons spread about the world and united in defense of our traditions, our way of life and of the world causes we and you espouse. If the population of the English-speaking commonwealth be added to that of the United States, with all that such co-operation implies in the air, on the sea and in science and industry, there will be no quivering, precarious balance of power to offer its temptation to ambition or adventure. On the contrary, there will be an overwhelming assurance of security. If we adhere faithfully to the charter of the United Nations and walk forward in sedate and sober strength, seeking no one's land or treasure, or seeking to lay no arbitrary control on the thoughts of men, if all British moral and material forces and convictions are joined with your own in fraternal association, the highroads of the future will be clear, not only for us but for all, not only for our time but for a century to come.

In 1947 Britain informed the United States that she could no longer support the Greeks in their fight against a communist insurrection supported from the outside. On March 12 of that year President Truman went before Congress and asked for legislation to undertake the support of both

Greece and Turkey, which was also in danger. The Truman Doctrine marked a new step in American involvement in world affairs.

Message of the President to the Congress

Mr. President, Mr. Speaker, Members of the Congress of the United States:

THE GRAVITY OF THE SITUATION which confronts the world today necessitates my appearance before a joint session of the Congress.

The foreign policy and the national security of this country are involved.

One aspect of the present situation, which I wish to present to you at this time for your consideration and decision, concerns Greece and Turkey.

The United States has received from the Greek Government an urgent appeal for financial and economic assistance. Preliminary reports from the American Economic Mission now in Greece and reports from the American Ambassador in Greece corroborate the statement of the Greek Government that assistance is imperative if Greece is to survive as a free nation.

I do not believe that the American people and the Congress wish to turn a deaf ear to the appeal of the Greek Government.

Greece is not a rich country. Lack of sufficient natural resources has always forced the Greek people to work hard to make both ends met. Since 1940 this industrious and peace-loving country has suffered invasion, four years of cruel enemy occupation, and bitter internal strife.

When forces of liberation entered Greece they found that the retreating Germans had destroyed virtually all the railways, roads, port facilities, communications, and merchant marine. More than a thousand villages had been burned. Eighty-five percent of the children were tubercular. Livestock, poultry, and draft animals had almost disappeared. Inflation had wiped out practically all savings.

As a result of these tragic conditions, a militant minority, exploiting human want and misery, was able to create political chaos which, until now, has made economic recovery impossible.

Greece is today without funds to finance the importation of those goods which are essential to bare subsistence. Under these circumstances the people of Greece cannot make progress in solving their problems of reconstruction. Greece is in desperate need of financial and economic assistance to enable it to

---

Senate Committee on Foreign Relations, *A Decade of American Foreign Policy: Basic Documents 1941–1949* (1950), pp. 1235–7.

resume purchases of food, clothing, fuel, and seeds. These are indispensable for the subsistence of its people and are obtainable only from abroad. Greece must have help to import the goods necessary to restore internal order and security so essential for economic and political recovery.

The Greek Government has also asked for the assistance of experienced American administrators, economists, and technicians to insure that the financial and other aid given to Greece shall be used effectively in creating a stable and self-sustaining economy and in improving its public administration.

The very existence of the Greek state is today threatened by the terrorist activities of several thousand armed men, led by Communists, who defy the Government's authority at a number of points, particularly along the northern boundaries. A commission appointed by the United Nations Security Council is at present investigating disturbed conditions in northern Greece and alleged border violations along the frontier between Greece on the one hand and Albania, Bulgaria, and Yugoslavia on the other.

Meanwhile, the Greek Government is unable to cope with the situation. The Greek Army is small and poorly equipped. It needs supplies and equipment if it is to restore authority to the Government throughout Greek territory.

Greece must have assistance if it is to become a self-supporting and self-respecting democracy.

The United States must supply that assistance. We have already extended to Greece certain types of relief and economic aid, but these are inadequate.

There is no other country to which democratic Greece can turn.

No other nation is willing and able to provide the necessary support for a democratic Greek Government.

The British Government, which has been helping Greece, can give no further financial or economic aid after March 31. Great Britain finds itself under the necessity of reducing or liquidating its commitments in several parts of the world, including Greece.

We have considered how the United Nations might assist in this crisis. But the situation is an urgent one requiring immediate action, and the United Nations and its related organizations are not in a position to extend help of the kind that is required.

It is important to note that the Greek Government has asked for our aid in utilizing effectively the financial and other assistance we may give to Greece, and in improving its public administration. It is of the utmost importance that we supervise the use of any funds made available to Greece, in such a manner that each dollar spent will count toward making Greece self-supporting, and will help to build an economy in which a healthy democracy can flourish.

No government is perfect. One of the chief virtues of a democracy, however, is that its defects are always visible and under democratic processes can be pointed out and corrected. The Government of Greece is not perfect. Nevertheless it represents 85 percent of the members of the Greek Parliament who were chosen in an election last year. Foreign observers, including 692 Americans, considered this election to be a fair expression of the views of the Greek people.

The Greek Government has been operating in an atmosphere of chaos and extremism. It has made mistakes. The extension of aid by this country does not mean that the United States condones everything that the Greek Government has done or will do. We have condemned in the past, and we condemn now, extremist measures of the right or the left. We have in the past advised tolerance, and we advise tolerance now.

Greece's neighbor, Turkey, also deserves our attention.

The future of Turkey as an independent and economically sound state is clearly no less important to the freedom-loving peoples of the world than the future of Greece. The circumstances in which Turkey finds itself today are considerably different from those of Greece. Turkey has been spared the disasters that have beset Greece. And during the war the United States and Great Britain furnished Turkey with material aid.

Nevertheless, Turkey now needs our support.

Since the war Turkey has sought additional financial assistance from Great Britain and the United States for the purpose of effecting that modernization necessary for the maintenance of its national integrity.

That integrity is essential to the preservation of order in the Middle East.

The British Government has informed us that, owing to its own difficulties, it can no longer extend financial or economic aid to Turkey.

As in the case of Greece, if Turkey is to have the assistance it needs, the United States must supply it. We are the only country able to provide that help.

I am fully aware of the broad implications involved if the United States extends assistance to Greece and Turkey, and I shall discuss these implications with you at this time.

One of the primary objectives of the foreign policy of the United States is the creation of conditions in which we and other nations will be able to work out a way of life free from coercion. This was a fundamental issue in the war with Germany and Japan. Our victory was won over countries which sought to impose their will, and their way of life, upon other nations.

To insure the peaceful development of nations, free from coercion, the United States has taken a leading part in establishing the United Nations. The United Nations is designed to make possible lasting freedom and independence for all its members. We shall not realize our objectives, however, unless we are willing to help free peoples to maintain their free institutions and their national integrity against aggressive movements that seek to impose upon them totalitarian regimes. This is no more than a frank recognition that totalitarian regimes imposed upon free peoples, by direct or indirect aggression, undermine the foundations of international peace and hence the security of the United States.

The peoples of a number of countries of the world have recently had totalitarian regimes forced upon them against their will. The Government of the United States has made frequent protests against coercion and intimidation, in violation of the Yalta agreement, in Poland, Rumania, and Bulgaria. I must also state that in a number of other countries there have been similar developments.

At the present moment in world history nearly every nation must choose between alternative ways of life. The choice is too often not a free one.

One way of life is based upon the will of the majority, and is distinguished by free institutions, representative government, free elections, guaranties, of individual liberty, freedom of speech and religion, and freedom from political oppression.

The second way of life is based upon the will of a minority forcibly imposed upon the majority. It relies upon terror and oppression, a controlled press and radio, fixed elections, and the suppression of personal freedoms.

I believe that it must be the policy of the United States to support free peoples who are resisting attempted subjugation by armed minorities or by outside pressures.

I believe that we must assist free peoples to work out their own destinies in their own way.

I believe that our help should be primarily through economic and financial aid which is essential to economic stability and orderly political processes.

The world is not static, and the *status quo* is not sacred. But we cannot allow changes in the *status quo* in violation of the Charter of the United Nations by such methods as coercion, or by such subterfuges as political infiltration. In helping free and independent nations to maintain their freedom, the United States will be giving effect to the principles of the Charter of the United Nations.

It is necessary only to glance at a map to realize that the survival and integrity of the Greek nation are of grave importance in a much wider situation. If Greece should fall under the control of an armed minority, the effect upon its neighbor, Turkey, would be immediate and serious. Confusion and disorder might well spread throughout the entire Middle East.

Moreover, the disappearance of Greece as an independent state would have a profound effect upon those countries in Europe whose peoples are struggling against great difficulties to maintain their freedoms and their independence while they repair the damages of war.

It would be an unspeakable tragedy if these countries, which have struggled so long against overwhelming odds, should lose that victory for which they sacrificed so much. Collapse of free institutions and loss of independence would be disastrous not only for them but for the world. Discouragement and possibly failure would quickly be the lot of neighboring peoples striving to maintain their freedom and independence.

Should we fail to aid Greece and Turkey in this fateful hour, the effect will be far-reaching to the West as well as to the East.

We must take immediate and resolute action.

I therefore ask the Congress to provide authority for assistance to Greece and Turkey in the amount of $400,000,000 for the period ending June 30, 1948. In requesting these funds, I have taken into consideration the maximum amount of relief assistance which would be furnished to Greece out of the $350,000,000 which I recently requested that the Congress authorize for the prevention of starvation and suffering in countries devastated by the war.

In addition to funds, I ask the Congress to authorize the detail of American civilian and military personnel to Greece and Turkey, at the request of those countries, to assist in the tasks of reconstruction, and for the purpose of supervising the use of such financial and material assistance as may be furnished. I recommend that authority also be provided for the instruction and training of selected Greek and Turkish personnel.

Finally, I ask that the Congress provide authority which will permit the speediest and most effective use, in terms of needed commodities, supplies, and equipment, of such funds as may be authorized.

If further funds, or further authority, should be needed for purposes indicated in this message, I shall not hesitate to bring the situation before the Congress. On this subject the Executive and Legislative branches of the Government must work together.

This is a serious course upon which we embark.

I would not recommend it except that the alternative is much more serious.

The United States contributed $341,000,000,000 toward winning World War II. This is an investment in world freedom and world peace.

The assistance that I am recommending for Greece and Turkey amounts to little more than one-tenth of one percent of this investment. It is only common sense that we should safeguard this investment and make sure that it was not in vain.

The seeds of totalitarian regimes are nurtured by misery and want. They spread and grow in the evil soil of poverty and strife. They reach their full growth when the hope of a people for a better life has died.

We must keep that hope alive.

The free peoples of the world look to us for support in maintaining their freedoms.

If we falter in our leadership, we may endanger the peace of the world— and we shall surely endanger the welfare of our own Nation.

Great responsibilities have been placed upon us by the swift movement of events.

I am confident that the Congress will face these responsibilities squarely.

The Russians did not fail to respond to the Truman Doctrine. The following editorial from Izvestia *presents their view.*

Editorial From Izvestia

ON MARCH 12, President Truman addressed a message to the U. S. Congress asking for 400 million dollars to be assigned for urgent aid to Greece and Turkey, and for authority to send to those countries American civil and military personnel, and to provide for the training by Americans by specially picked Greek and Turkish personnel.

Greece, said Truman, was in a desperate economic and political situation. Britain was no longer able to act as trustee for the Greeks. Turkey had requested speedy American aid. Turkey, unlike Greece, had not suffered from the Second World War, but she needed financial aid from Britain and from the U.S.A. in order to carry out that modernisation necessary for maintaining her national integrity. Since the British Government, on account of its own difficulties, was not capable of offering financial or other aid to the Turks, this aid must be furnished by the U.S.A.

Thus Congress was asked to do two "good deeds" at once—to save Greece from internal disorders and to pay for the cost of "modernising" Turkey.

The pathetic appeal of the Tsaldaris Government to the U.S.A. is clear evidence of the bankruptcy of the political regime in Greece. But the matter does not lie solely with the Greek Monarchists and their friends, now cracked up to American Congressmen as the direct descendents of the heroes of Thermopylae: it is well known that the real masters of Greece have been and are the British military authorities.

British troops have been on Greek territory since 1944. On Churchill's initiative, Britain took on herself the responsibility for "stabilising" political conditions in Greece. The British authorities did not confine themselves to perpetuating the rule of the reactionary, anti-democratic forces in Greece, making no scruple in supporting ex-collaborators with the Germans. The entire political and economic activities under a number of short-lived Greek Governments have been carried on under close British control and direction.

Today we can see the results of this policy—complete bankruptcy. British troops failed to bring peace and tranquillity to tormented Greece. The Greek people have been plunged into the abyss of new sufferings, of hunger and poverty. Civil war takes on ever fiercer forms.

Izvestia, March 13, 1947, in William A. Williams, *The Shaping of American Diplomacy* (1956), pp. 1003–5.

Was not the presence of foreign troops on Greek territory instrumental in bringing about this state of affairs? Does not Britain, who proclaimed herself the guardian of Greece, bear responsibility for the bankruptcy of her charge?

The American President's message completely glosses over these questions. The U.S.A. does not wish to criticise Britain, since she herself intends to follow the British example. Truman's statement makes it clear that the U.S.A. does not intend to deviate from the course of British policy in Greece. So one cannot expect better results.

The U. S. Government has no intention of acting in the Greek question as one might have expected a member of UNO, concerned about the fate of another member, to act. It is obvious that in Washington they do not wish to take into account the obligations assumed by the U. S. Government regarding UNO. Truman did not even consider it necessary to wait for the findings of the Security Council Commission specially sent to Greece to investigate the situation on the spot.

Truman, indeed, failed to reckon either with the international organisation or with the sovereignty of Greece. What will be left of Greek sovereignty when the "American military and civilian personnel" gets to work in Greece by means of the 250 million dollars brought into that country? The sovereignty and independence of Greece will be the first victims of such singular "defence."

The American arguments for assisting Turkey base themselves on the existence of a threat to the integrity of Turkish territory—though no-one and nothing actually threatens Turkey's integrity. This "assistance" is evidently aimed at putting this country also under U. S. control.

Some American commentators admit this quite openly. Walter Lippmann, for example, frankly points out in the *Herald Tribune* that an American alliance with Turkey would give the U.S.A. a strategic position, incomparably more advantageous than any other, from which power could be wielded over the Middle East.

Commenting on Truman's message to Congress, the *New York Times* proclaims the advent of "the age of American responsibility." Yet what is this responsibility but a smokescreen for expansion? The cry of saving Greece and Turkey from the expansion of the so-called "totalitarian states" is not new. Hitler used to refer to the Bolsheviks when he wanted to open the road for his own conquests. Now they want to take Greece and Turkey under their control, they raise a din about "totalitarian states." This seems all the more attractive since, in elbowing in itself, the U.S.A. is pushing non-totalitarian Britain out of yet another country or two.

We are now witnessing a fresh intrusion of the U.S.A. into the affairs of other states. American claims to leadership in international affairs grow parallel with the growing appetite of the American quarters concerned. But the American leaders, in the new historical circumstances, fail to reckon with the fact that the old methods of the colonisers and diehard politicians have out-lived their time and are doomed to failure. In this lies the chief weakness of Truman's message.

Aware that the threat of communist revolution was greatest where poverty existed, Secretary of State Marshall proposed a plan whereby the United States would help the European nations return to prosperity. Although the Iron Curtain countries were included in the Marshall Plan, Russian hostility prevented their participation.

The European Recovery Program

REMARKS BY SECRETARY MARSHALL, JUNE 5, 1947

I NEED NOT TELL YOU GENTLEMEN that the world situation is very serious. That must be apparent to all intelligent people. I think one difficulty is that the problem is one of such enormous complexity that the very mass of facts presented to the public by press and radio make it exceedingly difficult for the man in the street to reach a clear appraisement of the situation. Furthermore, the people of this country are distant from the troubled areas of the earth and it is hard for them to comprehend the plight and consequent reactions of the long-suffering peoples, and the effect of those reactions on their governments in connection with our efforts to promote peace in the world.

In considering the requirements for the rehabilitation of Europe, the physical loss of life, the visible destruction of cities, factories, mines, and railroads was correctly estimated, but it has become obvious during recent months that this visible destruction was probably less serious than the dislocation of the entire fabric of European economy. For the past 10 years conditions have been highly abnormal. The feverish preparation for war and the more feverish maintenance of the war effort engulfed all aspects of national economies. Machinery has fallen into disrepair or is entirely obsolete. Under the arbitrary and destructive Nazi rule, virtually every possible enterprise was geared into the German war machine. Long-standing commercial ties, private institutions, banks, insurance companies, and shipping companies disappeared, through loss of capital, absorption through nationalization, or by simple destruction. In many countries, confidence in the local

Senate Committee on Foreign Relations, *A Decade of American Foreign Policy: Basic Documents, 1941–1949* (1950), pp. 1268–70.

currency has been severely shaken. The breakdown of the business structure of Europe during the war was complete. Recovery has been seriously retarded by the fact that two years after the close of hostilities a peace settlement with Germany and Austria has not been agreed upon. But even given a more prompt solution of these difficult problems, the rehabilitation of the economic structure of Europe quite evidently will require a much longer time and greater effort than had been foreseen.

There is a phase of this matter which is both interesting and serious. The farmer has always produced the foodstuffs to exchange with the city dweller for the other necessities of life. This division of labor is the basis of modern civilization. At the present time it is threatened with breakdown. The town and city industries are not producing adequate goods to exchange with the food-producing farmer. Raw materials and fuel are in short supply. Machinery is lacking or worn out. The farmer or the peasant cannot find the goods for sale which he desires to purchase. So the sale of his farm produce for money which he cannot use seems to him an unprofitable transaction. He, therefore, has withdrawn many fields from crop cultivation and is using them for grazing. He feeds more grain to stock and finds for himself and his family an ample supply of food, however short he may be on clothing and the other ordinary gadgets of civilization. Meanwhile people in the cities are short of food and fuel. So the governments are forced to use their foreign money and credits to procure these necessities abroad. This process exhausts funds which are urgently needed for reconstruction. Thus a very serious situation is rapidly developing which bodes no good for the world. The modern system of the division of labor upon which the exchange of products is based is in danger of breaking down.

The truth of the matter is that Europe's requirements for the next three or four years of foreign food and other essential products—principally from America—are so much greater than her present ability to pay that she must have substantial additional help or face economic, social, and political deterioration of a very grave character.

The remedy lies in breaking the vicious circle and restoring the confidence of the European people in the economic future of their own countries and of Europe as a whole. The manufacturer and the farmer throughout wide areas must be able and willing to exchange their products for currencies the continuing value of which is not open to question.

Aside from the demoralizing effect on the world at large and the possibilities of disturbances arising as a result of the desperation of the people concerned, the consequences to the economy of the United States should be apparent to all. It is logical that the United States should do whatever it is able to do to assist in the return of normal economic health in the world, without which there can be no political stability and no assured peace. Our policy is directed not against any country or doctrine but against hunger, poverty, desperation, and chaos. Its purpose should be the revival of a working economy in the world so as to permit the emergence of political and social conditions in which free institutions can exist. Such assistance, I am convinced, must not be on a piecemeal basis as various crises develop. Any assistance that this Government may render in the future should provide a cure rather than a mere palliative. Any government that is willing to assist in the task of recovery will find full cooperation, I am sure, on the part of the United States Government. Any government which maneuvers to block the recovery of other countries cannot expect help from us. Furthermore, governments, political parties, or groups which seek to perpetuate human misery in order to profit therefrom politically or otherwise will encounter the opposition of the United States.

It is already evident that, before the United States Government can proceed much further in its efforts to alleviate the situation and help start the European world on its way to recovery, there must be some agreement among the countries of Europe as to the requirements of the situation and the part those countries themselves will take in order to give proper effect to whatever action might be undertaken by this Government. It would be neither fitting nor efficacious for this Government to undertake to draw up unilaterally a program designed to place Europe on its feet economically. This is the business of the Europeans. The initiative, I think, must come from Europe. The role of this country should consist of friendly aid in the drafting of a European program and of later support of such a program so far as it may be practical for us to do so. The program should be a joint one, agreed to by a number, if not all, European nations.

An essential part of any successful action on the part of the United States is an understanding on the part of the people of America of the character of the problem and the remedies to be applied. Political passion and prejudice should have no part. With foresight, and a willingness on the part of our people to face up to the vast responsibility which history has clearly placed upon our country, the difficulties I have outlined can and will be overcome.

In February, 1948, democratic Czechoslovakia experienced a Communist coup d'état, which effectively made it a Russian satellite. The following correspondence between President Beneš and the Communist Party clearly indicates the course of events.

FROM *President Beneš' Correspondence with the Presidium of the Communist Party*

Letter from President Beneš to Presidium of the Communist Party

February 24, 1948

YOU SENT ME A LETTER on February 21 in which you express your attitude on a solution of the crisis and ask me to agree with it. Allow me to formulate my own attitude.

I feel fully the great responsibility of this fateful hour on our national and state life. From the beginning of this crisis I have been thinking about the situation as it was forming itself, putting these affairs of ours in connection with world affairs.

I am trying to see clearly not only the present situation but also the causes that led to it and the results that a decision can have. I am aware of the powerful forces through which the situation is being formed.

In a calm, matter of fact, impassionate and objective judgment of the situation I feel, through the common will of various groups of our citizens which turn their attention to me, that the will is expressed to maintain the peace and order and discipline voluntarily accepted to achieve a progressive and really socialist life.

How to achieve this goal? You know my sincerely democratic creed. I cannot but stay faithful to that creed even at this moment because democracy, according to my belief, is the only reliable and durable basis for a decent and dignified human life.

I insist on parliamentary democracy and parliamentary government as it limits democracy. I state I know very well it is necessary to social and economic content. I built my political work on these principles and cannot—without betraying myself—act otherwise.

The present crisis of democracy here too cannot be overcome but through democratic and parliamentary means. I thus do not overlook your

The Strategy and Tactics of World Communism, Supplement III, *The Coup d'Etat in Prague*, House of Representatives Committee on Foreign Affairs, National and International Movements, Subcommittee No. 5 Report (1948), pp. 25–7.

demands. I regard all our political parties associated in the National Front as bearers of political responsibility. We all accepted the principle of the National Front and this proved successful up to the recent time when the crisis began.

This crisis, however, in my opinion, does not deny the principle in itself. I am convinced that on this principle, even in the future, the necessary cooperation of all can be achieved. All disputes can be solved for the benefit of the national and common state of the Czechs and the Slovaks.

I therefore have been in negotiation with five political parties. I have listened to their views and some of them also have been put in writing. These are grave matters and I cannot ignore them.

Therefore, I again have to appeal to all to find a peaceful solution and new successful cooperation through parliamentary means and through the National Front.

That much for the formal side. As far as the personal side is concerned, it is clear to me, as I have said already, that the Prime Minister will be the chairman of the strongest party element, Gottwald.

Finally, on the factual side of this matter it is clear to me that socialism is a way of life desired by an overwhelming part of our nation. At the same time I believe that with socialism a certain measure of freedom and unity is possible and that these are vital principles to all in our national life.

Our nation has struggled for freedom almost throughout its history. History also has shown us where discord can lead.

I beg of you therefore to relive these facts and make them the starting point for our negotiations. Let us all together begin negotiations again for further durable cooperation and let us not allow prolongation of the split of the nation into two quarreling parts.

I believe that a reasonable agreement is possible because it is indispensable.

Reply by the Presidium of the Communist Party to Letter of President Beneš

February 25, 1948

The Presidium of the Central Committee of the Communist Party acknowledges your letter dated February 24 and states again that it cannot enter into negotiations with the present leadership of the National Socialist, People's and Slovak Democratic Parties because this would not conform to the interests of the unity of the people nor with the interests of further peaceful development of the republic.

Recent events indisputably proved that these three parties no longer represent the interests of the working people of the cities and countryside, that their leaders have betrayed the fundamental ideas of the people's democracy and National Front as they have been stated by the Kosice Government program and that they assumed the position of undermining the opposition.

This was shown again and again in the government, in the Constitutional National Assembly, in the press of these parties, and in actions that, with menacing levity, were organized by their central secretariats against the interests of the working people, against the security of the state, against the alliances of the republic, against state finance, against nationalized industry, against urgent agricultural reforms—in one word, against the whole constructive efforts of our people and against the very foundations, internal and external, of the security of the country.

These parties even got in touch with foreign circles hostile to our people's democratic order and our alliances, and in collaboration with these hostile foreign elements they attempted disruption of the present development of the republic.

This constantly increasing activity was crowned by an attempt to break up the government, an attempt that, as it was proved, should have been accompanied by actions aiming at a putsch.

Massive people's manifestations during the last few days clearly have shown our working people denounce, with complete unity and with indignation, the policy of these parties and ask the creation of a government in which all honest progressive patriots devoted to the republic and the people are represented.

Also among the members of the above-mentioned three parties an increasing amount of indignation can be seen. The members ask for a rebirth of their own parties and the National Front.

In conformity with this powerfully expressed will of the people, the Presidium of the Central Committee of the Communist Party approved the proposals of Premier Klement Gottwald according to which the government will be filled in with prominent representatives of all parties and also big nation-wide organizations.

We stress that a government filled in this way will present itself, with full agreement with the principles of parliamentary democracy, before the Constitutional National Assembly with its program and ask for its approval.

Being convinced that only such a highly constitutional and parliamentary process can guarantee the peaceful development of the republic and at the same time it corresponds to the ideas of a complete majority of the working people, the Presidium of the Central Committee hopes firmly after careful consideration that you will recognize the correctness of its conclusions and will agree with its proposals.

In 1949 the United States abandoned its traditional hostility toward entangling alliances and joined the North Atlantic Treaty Organization to counter Soviet pressure against

Western Europe. It was the decisive recognition that the Cold War was to be a lasting reality.

North Atlantic Treaty

THE PARTIES TO THIS TREATY reaffirm their faith in the purposes and principles of the Charter of the United Nations and their desire to live in peace with all peoples and all governments.

They are determined to safeguard the freedom, common heritage and civilization of their peoples, founded on the principles of democracy, individual liberty and the rule of law.

They seek to promote stability and well-being in the North Atlantic area.

They are resolved to unite their efforts for collective defense and for the preservation of peace and security.

They therefore agree to this North Atlantic Treaty:

ARTICLE 1

The Parties undertake, as set forth in the Charter of the United Nations, to settle any international disputes in which they may be involved by peaceful means in such a manner that international peace and security, and justice, are not endangered, and to refrain in their international relations from the threat or use of force in any manner inconsistent with the purposes of the United Nations.

ARTICLE 2

The Parties will contribute toward the further development of peaceful and friendly international relations by strengthening their free institutions, by bringing about a better understanding of the principles upon which these institutions are founded, and by promoting conditions of stability and well-being. They will seek to eliminate conflict in their international economic policies and will encourage economic collaboration between any or all of them.

ARTICLE 3

In order more effectively to achieve the objectives of this Treaty, the Parties, separately and jointly, by means of continuous and effective self-help and mutual aid, will maintain and develop their individual and collective capacity to resist armed attack.

Senate Committee on Foreign Relations, *A Decade of American Foreign Policy: Basic Documents, 1941–1949* (1950), pp. 1328–31.

ARTICLE 4

The Parties will consult together whenever, in the opinion of any of them, the territorial integrity, political independence or security of any of the Parties is threatened.

ARTICLE 5

The Parties agree that an armed attack against one or more of them in Europe or North America shall be considered an attack against them all; and consequently they agree that, if such an armed attack occurs, each of them, in exercise of the right of individual or collective self-defense recognized by Article 51 of the Charter of the United Nations, will assist the Party or Parties so attacked by taking forthwith, individually and in concert with the other Parties, such action as it deems necessary, including the use of armed force, to restore and maintain the security of the North Atlantic area.

Any such armed attack and all measures taken as a result thereof shall immediately be reported to the Security Council. Such measures shall be terminated when the Security Council has taken the measures necessary to restore and maintain international peace and security.

ARTICLE 6

For the purpose of Article 5 an armed attack on one or more of the Parties is deemed to include an armed attack on the territory of any of the Parties in Europe or North America, on the Algerian departments of France, on the occupation forces of any Party in Europe, on the islands under the jurisdiction of any Party in the North Atlantic area north of the Tropic of Cancer or on the vessels or aircraft in this area of any of the Parties.

ARTICLE 7

This Treaty does not affect, and shall not be interpreted as affecting, in any way the rights and obligations under the Charter of the Parties which are members of the United Nations, or the primary responsibility of the Security Council for the maintenance of international peace and security.

ARTICLE 8

Each Party declares that none of the international engagements now in force between it and any other of the Parties or any third state is in conflict with the provisions of this Treaty, and undertakes not to enter into any international engagement in conflict with this Treaty.

ARTICLE 9

The Parties hereby established a council, on which each of them shall be represented, to consider matters concerning the implementation of this Treaty. The council shall be so organized as to be able to meet promptly at any time. The council shall set up such subsidiary bodies as may be necessary; in particular it shall establish immediately a defense committee which shall recommend measures for the implementation of Articles 3 and 5.

ARTICLE 10

The Parties may, by unanimous agreement, invite any other European state in a position to further the principles of this Treaty and to contribute to the security of the North Atlantic area to accede to this Treaty. Any state so invited may become a party to the Treaty by depositing its instrument of accession with the Government of the United States of America. The Government of the United States of America will inform each of the Parties of the deposit of each such instrument of accession.

ARTICLE 11

This Treaty shall be ratified and its provisions carried out by the Parties in accordance with their respective constitutional processes. The instruments of ratification shall be deposited as soon as possible with the Government of the United States of America, which will notify all the other signatories of each deposit. The Treaty shall enter into force between the states which have ratified it as soon as the ratifications of the majority of the signatories, including the ratifications of Belgium, Canada, France, Luxembourg, the Netherlands, the United Kingdom and the United States, have been deposited and shall come into effect with respect to other states on the date of the deposit of their ratifications.

ARTICLE 12

After the Treaty has been in force for ten years, or at any time thereafter, the Parties shall, if any of them so requests, consult together for the purpose of reviewing the Treaty, having regard for the factors then affecting peace and security in the North Atlantic area, including the development of universal as well as regional arrangements under the Charter of the United Nations for the maintenance of international peace and security.

ARTICLE 13

After the Treaty has been in force for twenty years, any Party may cease to be a party one year after its notice of denunciation has been given to the Government of the United States of America, which will inform the Governments of the other Parties of the deposit of each notice of denunciation.

ARTICLE 14

This Treaty, of which the English and French texts are equally authentic, shall be deposited in the archives of the Government of the United States of America. Duly certified copies thereof will be transmitted by that Government to the Governments of the other signatories.

In witness whereof, the undersigned plenipotentiaries have signed this Treaty.

Done at Washington, the fourth day of April, 1949.

For the Kingdom of Belgium:
P. H. Spaak
Silvercruys

For Canada:
Lester B. Pearson
H. H. Wrong

For the Kingdom of Denmark:
Gustav Rasmussen
Henrik Kauffmann

For France:
Schuman
H. Bonnet

For Iceland:
Bjarni Benediktsson
Thor Thors

For Italy:
Sforza
Alberto Tarchiani

For the Grand Duchy of Luxembourg:
Jos Bech
Hugues Le Gallais

For the Kingdom of the Netherlands:
Stikker
E. N. Van Kleffens

For the Kingdom of Norway:
Halvard M. Lange
Wilhelm Munthe Morgenstierne

For Portugal:
José Caeiro da Matta
Pedro Theotónio Pereira

For the United Kingdom of Great Britain and Northern Ireland:
Ernest Bevin
Oliver Franks

For the United States of America:
Dean Acheson

I certify that the foregoing is a true copy of the North Atlantic Treaty signed at Washington on April 4, 1949 in the English and French languages, the signed original of which is deposited in the archives of the Government of the United States of America.

In testimony whereof, I, Dean Acheson, Secretary of State of the United States of America, have hereunto caused the seal of the Department of State to be affixed and my name subscribed by the Authentication Officer of the said Department, at the city of Washington, in the District of Columbia, this fourth day of April, 1949.

DEAN ACHESON
Secretary of State
By M. P. CHAUVIN
Authentication Officer
Department of State

3 Russia's Responsibility

FROM *A Diplomatic History of the American People*

BY THOMAS A. BAILEY

> *We may well ask, "Why have they [the Soviets] deliberately acted for*
> *three long years so as to unite the free world against them?"*
>
> WINSTON CHURCHILL, 1949

UNFINISHED BUSINESS

URGENT PROBLEMS of an economic and humanitarian nature lay piled
on the tables of the diplomats when the war finally jarred to a close. "It is
now 11:59 on the clock of starvation," warned Herbert Hoover.

A temporary organization, the United Nations Relief and Rehabilitation
Administration (UNRRA), was launched late in 1943, when representatives
of forty-odd nations signed an agreement at the White House. Its primary
purpose was to help the liberated peoples of Europe and the Far East to get
back onto their feet. The uninvaded member nations were invited to contribute to the budget of UNRRA a small percentage of their incomes in 1943.
The United States, as the wealthiest participant, became the chief financial
backer and leader of this vast humanitarian enterprise. When the books were
closed in 1947, huge quantities of urgently needed food and other supplies
had been shipped to China and the nations of Europe, notably Poland, Italy,
Yugoslavia, Czechoslovakia, Greece, and Austria.

Hardly less clamorous was the problem of the several million Displaced
Persons (DP's), all of whom had been uprooted by the war and many of
whom dared not return to their Communist-enslaved homelands. The
American people were more generous in sending money to Europe than they
were in inviting the impoverished peoples of Europe to their shores. Painful
memories of unemployment during the Great Depression were still fresh.
Finally, in June, 1948, Congress made a belated beginning when it voted to
set aside quota restrictions and admit 205,000. The treatment of these DP's—
Delayed Pilgrims, someone has called them—was harshly criticized as over-

From *A Diplomatic History of the American People*, Seventh Edition, pp. 776–9, 790–1,
796–803, 807–9, by Thomas A. Bailey. Copyright © 1964 by Meredith Publishing Company.
Reprinted by permission of Appleton-Century-Crofts, Division of Meredith Publishing Company.

cautious, and the sifting process was widely condemned as discriminating against Catholics and Jews.

The settlement of lend-lease obligations, on the other hand, presented a far prettier picture than the prolonged wrangling over Allied debts after World War I. The total account at the end of World War II was approximately $50 billion, of which about $31 billion had gone to the British Empire and $11 billion to the Soviet Union. This staggering total was reduced some $10 billion by reverse-lend lease—that is, the supplying of goods or services for the United States at the other end. By late 1953, adjustments had been threshed out with all the major debtors, except the Soviet Union. As of that date, the settlement agreements had reduced the total to be paid to about $1 billion, which amounted to approximately three cents on the dollar.

The liquidation of the lend-lease account was both more generous and more realistic than that of the war-debt account following World War I. The original lend-lease agreements had stipulated that the ultimate terms should "promote mutually advantageous economic relations." Happily, this far-visioned formula was generally followed in making the necessary reductions.

THE COMMUNIST CHALLENGE

When the war ended with an atomic bang in 1945, the American people still retained a vast reservoir of good will toward their valiant Russian ally. He had saved their hides while saving his own. Not only were Americans counting on Soviet co-operation to create a warless world, but many of them favored lending Russia money and technical assistance to repair the ravages inflicted by the Nazi invader.

But the Kremlin brutally slapped aside the outstretched American hand, presumably because co-operation with the capitalistic West would retard the Communist revolution. The ideal of One World thus collided head on with the actuality of the Communist world. The resulting deadlock was the most momentous and terrifying single development of the postwar years.

By the summer of 1946, if not earlier, the various public opinion polls in the United States revealed disquieting conclusions. The American people did not regard Russia as a peace-loving nation, and they did not trust her to co-operate with the United Nations. Her dominance over her satellite neighbors, they felt, was prompted by aggressive rather than defensive designs, and they were convinced that the Kremlin was bent on enchaining the entire globe. Not only was another war probable within twenty-five years, most Americans believed, but the Russians were the most likely to start it.

The Soviets thus unwittingly engineered a psychological Pearl Harbor. Crying "capitalist encirclement," they were bolstering their armed forces while the democracies were demobilizing theirs. Within a few short months the aggressive tactics of Moscow had awakened the American people to the true nature of the Communist conspiracy. Thus forewarned and alerted, the

United States undertook to revamp its foreign policies and bolster its defenses in a determined effort not to be caught napping again.

THE BLAME FOR THE BREAK

Who was responsible for the shattered dream of One World? Apologists for Russia have insisted that the Soviets turned against America because America first turned against them. They further allege—the Myth of the Empty Chair—that if Roosevelt had not come to an untimely end, he would have been able to co-operate with the Kremlin.

The naked truth is that by mid-March, 1945—one month before the President's death—the Soviets were clearly taking over Poland and Romania as satellites in violation of their solemn pledges at Yalta. Roosevelt died knowing, or strongly suspecting, that he had failed in his gigantic gamble to wean Stalin away from his dangerous ideals by kind words and lend-lease largesse. The Russian leaders, although soft-pedaling Communist world revolution during the desperate days of World War II, had never really abandoned it. They had cleverly deceived the Americans, who in turn were in a mood to deceive themselves.

American military strategy, moreover, played directly into the hands of the Soviets. The forward-dashing American columns might have captured Berlin and Prague after costly fighting. But pursuant in part to arrangements made earlier with the Soviets, the Red Armies were allowed to enter these capitals as liberator-conquerors. The Americans kept their agreements, while hoping that the Russians, despite mounting evidence to the contrary, would keep theirs. The "liberating" Reds thus further entrenched themselves on the soil of the neighboring satellites.

Less defensible was the overhasty withdrawal of the American armies from Europe, and the consequent creation of a power vacuum into which the Soviets speedily moved. Short-sightedly assuming that victory is self-perpetuating, and that wars end with the shooting, the American public demanded a speedy dismantling of one of the most potent striking forces ever assembled. Roosevelt himself was privately committed to bringing the troops home at the earliest possible date. The men in uniform staged incredible "I Wanna Go Home" demonstrations, and they were backed to the hilt by lonesome wives, mothers, sweethearts, and children ("Bring-Daddy-Back-Home" clubs). As in 1918, the American fire department withdrew before the fire was completely out. Winston Churchill expressed the opinion in 1949 that only the existence of the atomic bomb, a temporary monopoly of the Americans, kept the Soviets from sweeping to the English channel.

The atomic bomb—a veritable apple of discord—aroused genuine fear in the Soviet Union. A tiny but vocal group of Americans, including ex-Governor Earle of Pennsylvania, was demanding a "preventive war" while the United States had this frightful new weapon and the Soviet Union did not.

The "rattling of the atomic bomb" became louder when American forces retained bomber bases within striking distance of Russia's industrial vitals, and undertook impressive naval demonstrations in the Mediterranean. Soviet suspicions deepened as Washington delayed or halted lend-lease shipments, and as the American public grew increasingly cold toward a proposed postwar loan of $6 billion.

THE IRON CURTAIN CLANGS DOWN

The oft-invaded Russians were determined to strengthen themselves against future foes by marshaling subservient satellite nations on their flanks. The descent of Moscow's "iron curtain" around the neighbors of the Soviet Union aroused the American people, more than anything else, to the nature of the Communist peril.

Soviet darkness gradually enshrouded Romania, Bulgaria, Albania, and Hungary, as Moscow-manipulated stooges took command. Washington, appealing to Stalin's unredeemed pledges at Yalta, lodged repeated protests with Moscow against coercion and intimidation. But in Soviet thinking security ranked higher than capitalistic conceptions of honor. Washington also made repeated representations to the satellites themselves—and with no greater success—against such offenses as the execution of political prisoners and the persecution of religious leaders.

Night likewise descended over Poland when a Soviet-dominated regime took control in 1945, also in defiance of Stalin's pledges at Yalta. After exasperating delays, the farcical "free and unfettered" election, also promised at Yalta, was held in 1947. The Communists polled about 90 per cent of the vote, although the American ambassador reported that in an honest election the opposition party would have won about 60 per cent of the votes. Washington's protests against the flouting of the Yalta pledges were wasted paper and ink.

Yugoslavia, a Communist satellite under the iron hand of Marshal Tito, presented special problems. The Yugoslavs reacted violently against America's opposition to their proposed grab of the Italian-Yugoslav city of Trieste, at the head of the Adriatic Sea. The internationalization of the city created a witches' cauldron, and numerous clashes ensued between the Yugoslav soldiers, on the one hand, and the American and British occupying troops, on the other.

The Western world breathed easier in 1948, when Tito parted company with Moscow, amid angry words. While still a Communist, he preferred his own local brand to that dictated by Moscow. Just as Roosevelt grasped the bloody hand of Stalin when he split with Hitler in 1941, so Truman grasped the bloody hand of Tito when he split with the Kremlin in 1948. In the hope of encouraging "Titoism" or independence among the other satellites of Moscow, the United States dispatched arms and supplies to Tito. In less than ten years these subventions amounted to about $2 billion, despite considerable opposition in America to underwriting any form of communism. As in the days of the Franco-American Alliance of 1778, a common danger was still making strange bedfellows.

Let us not be deceived—we are today in the midst of a cold war.

BERNARD BARUCH, April, 1947

THE TRUMAN DOCTRINE

The naked aggressions of Moscow had, by early 1947, swung American opinion around in favor of a "get-tough-with-Russia" policy. President Truman, aware of imminent Communist inroads and confident of strong public backing, prepared to take resolute action. As he privately remarked, "I'm tired of babying the Soviets."

The time for decision came in February, 1947. The overburdened British shocked Washington by announcing that they could no longer provide full-scale economic support for the "rightist" government of Greece. When they withdrew their assistance, the Communist guerrillas, who were receiving help from their Communist neighbors to the north, would no doubt seize control. Greece would then gravitate into the Soviet orbit. The position of Turkey, on which Moscow was exerting heavy pressure, would become untenable. The strategically vital eastern Mediterranean would presumably fall like a ripe pear into Communist hands, and the impact on the free world would be catastrophic.

President Truman, after hurried conferences with military and Congressional leaders, made a surprise appearance before Congress, on March 12, 1947, to present an epochal pronouncement. In solemn tones he described the plight of war-racked Greece, and then declared:

> One of the primary objectives of the foreign policy of the United States is the creation of conditions in which we and other nations will be able to work out a way of life free from coercion. . . . We shall not realize our objectives, however, unless we are willing to help free peoples to maintain their free institutions and their national integrity against aggressive movements that seek to impose upon them totalitarian regimes. [Applause.] This is no more than a frank recognition that totalitarian regimes imposed on free peoples, by direct or indirect aggression, undermine the foundations of international peace and hence the security of the United States.

Truman thereupon concluded that "it must be the policy of the United States to support free peoples who are resisting attempted subjugation by armed minorities or by outside pressures." With this goal in view, he requested an appropriation of $400 million for economic and military succor to Greece and Turkey. This, he conceded, was a "serious course," but the alternative to drifting was "much more serious. [Applause.]" The implication was clear that Congress had better expend a modest amount of the taxpayers' money than later expend the taxpayer himself. When Truman concluded, Congress arose as one man to applaud—except for one left-wing member.

CASH FOR "CONTAINMENT"

The Truman Doctrine was the major opening gun in what journalists called the "cold war"—a war waged by means other than shooting. It also inaugurated in a spectacular way the new policy of "containment" or the attempt to stem Soviet advances in vital spots. The public, though now willing to halt Russian aggression by risky measures, was momentarily stunned by the President's blast. But the feeling was general that while the "Truman Doctrine" was fraught with peril, a policy of dangerous do-nothingism was even more perilous. The only two major groups to express strong hostility were the left-wing "liberals," for whom Henry A. Wallace was a spokesman, and the old-line isolationists, for whom the *Chicago Tribune* was a leading mouthpiece.

Critics of the Truman Doctrine advanced numerous and weighty arguments. It would cost too much, for the initial appropriation would be but a drop in the bucket. It would create the bad precedent of sticking the national nose into the internal affairs of other nations. It would goad into war the Soviet Communists, who would not be fought with mere dollars. It would bypass the United Nations and weaken that organization at the very time when it was getting off to a wobbly start.

As far as the UN was concerned, Truman had clearly taken lone-hand action because of the inevitable delaying tactics of the Soviets. But he had gone so far out on the end of a limb that he could not be repudiated without weakening the United States in the eyes of the world at a critical hour. Senator Vandenberg of Michigan, who with a majority of his Republican colleagues continued to support a bipartisan foreign policy, helped to push through Congress a face-saving amendment. It stipulated that whenever the United Nations was prepared to take over the burden, the United States would lay it down.

After a windy debate of about two months, Congress approved the initial Truman Doctrine appropriation of $400 million on May 15, 1947. The vote, which reflected wide public support, was 67 to 23 in the Senate and 287 to 107 in the House.

The Truman Doctrine was of incalculable significance. It enabled the United States to seize the offensive in the "cold war" to "contain" communism. Although limited to Greece and Turkey, it was general in scope and led by direct steps to the vastly more important Marshall Plan and the North Atlantic Treaty Organization (NATO). It was a kind of lend-lease—this time against communism rather than fascism. It reversed the nonintervention principle of the original Monroe Doctrine, but like the Monroe Doctrine it aimed at long-range defense.

THE MARSHALL PLAN

Once the American people had accepted the principle of helping independent governments resist communism, they gradually perceived that stopgap aid for only Greece and Turkey was merely sending a boy on a man's errand. War-blasted Western Europe, further scourged by the icy winter of 1946–1947, was not making the necessary economic recovery. Local Communist groups were deliberately sabotaging progress by strikes and other incendiary tactics. If the chaos that was so favorable to communism should develop, the Communists would probably seize control of Italy and France. All Western Europe would then fall into their grip, and Moscow's influence would sweep to the English Channel.

Into the breach boldly stepped the Secretary of State, General Marshall. Speaking at the Harvard University commencement exercises, on June 5, 1947, he announced a policy that forthwith dwarfed the Truman Doctrine. He suggested that the nations of Europe get together, devise long-range plans for economic recovery, concentrate on self-help and mutual assistance, and present to Washington a specific statement of their needs. The United States would then support them with financial help "so far as it may be practical. . . ."

The Marshall speech did not at once make a great splash in the United States. It was not a clear-cut promise, and it put the burden of initiative squarely on Europe's shoulders. But gradually the American people perceived that the Marshall scheme was no unilateral Truman Doctrine aimed at military aid or temporary relief. It was an inclusive plan looking toward long-range rehabilitation.

The foreign ministers of France and Britain, recognizing the breathtaking implications of Marshall's overture, seized the initiative. They arranged for a meeting at Paris, to which the Soviet foreign minister, V. M. Molotov, was also invited. After a short but stormy stay, he finally walked out, thus spurning an enviable opportunity to tie up the Marshall Plan with obstructionism.

The British and French thereupon issued invitations for a general conference at Paris, to which twenty-two nations were invited—all Europe west of Russia except Fascist Spain. The eight nations under the shadow of the Kremlin declined, or were forced to spurn the "imperialist" plot, cooked up for "the enslavement of Europe." They were Albania, Bulgaria, Czechoslovakia, Finland, Hungary, Poland, Romania, and Yugoslavia. The sixteen that accepted were Austria, Belgium, Britain, Denmark, Eire, France, Greece, Iceland, Italy, Luxembourg, the Netherlands, Norway, Portugal, Sweden, Switzerland and Turkey. Representatives of these sixteen Marshall

Plan countries, meeting in Paris from July to September, 1947, finally wove their "shopping lists" of help desired from America into an integrated program.

One defiant answer of Moscow to the Marshall Plan was the nine-nation Communist Information Bureau (Cominform), announced on October 5, 1947. It was in effect a revival of the Old Comintern, which ostensibly had been disbanded in 1943. The new agency was openly designed to promote communism by sabotaging the economic recovery of Europe under the Marshall Plan. At the same time the Kremlin, through the counter Molotov Plan, would attempt to shackle its satellites together as an economie whole.

MARSHALING MARSHALL DOLLARS

The scene now shifted to Washington, where President Truman submitted his Marshall Plan estimates to Congress, in December, 1947. They embraced $17 billion for four-and-one-quarter years, with an initial outlay of $6.8 billion for the first fifteen months. The debate in Congress then began in earnest, and despite the urgent need for haste, consumed more than three precious months.

Advocates of the Marshall Plan, though appealing to simple humanitarianism, stressed the bread-and-butter argument that a prosperous Europe was essential for America's own prosperity. Industrial and agricultural groups, worried about their overseas markets, warmly seconded this view. But the necessity of halting Soviet communism was no doubt the compelling argument. The Marshall Plan was admittedly a calculated risk, but it was cheaper than war. If successful in redressing the European balance, it might head off a conflict that would be infinitely costly and destructive.

Critics of the Marshall scheme charged that it was just another "Operation Rathole." "Uncle Santa Claus" had already poured too much money into the pockets of ungrateful Europeans—about $12 billion in various loans and handouts since mid-1945. America had better make herself strong at home, conserve her resources, and help her own needy people. Otherwise she would offend the Soviets (who were already offended), divide Europe (which was already divided), and lay herself open to the Russian charge (which had already been made) of "dollar imperialism." The whole device, cried Henry A. Wallace, was a "Martial Plan."

The Kremlin unwittingly helped spur the languishing Marshall Plan appropriation through Congress. The Communist coup of February, 1948, in Czechoslovakia had a profound effect, especially the suicide of the beloved Foreign Minister Masaryk under circumstances that suggested foul play. Hardly less disturbing was Moscow's strong-arming of "Brave little" Finland into a distasteful alliance. These alarming developments not only increased enthusiasm for the Marshall Plan, but sped through Congress an unprecedented peacetime conscription law and an appropriation for a potent airforce.

The debate on Marshall aid at length ended. The legislators, who were unwilling to bind future Congresses by a long-term appropriation, finally voted $6.098 billion for various purposes during the first twelve months. The tacit understanding was that similar sums would be forthcoming through the next three years. This measure, after passing the House 329 to 74 and the Senate 69 to 19, was signed by Truman on April 3, 1948.

The Marshall Plan—officially known as the European Relief Program (ERP)—was approved just in time to influence the Italian election. The militant Communist Party, crying "Death to Truman" was threatening to seize control and undermine the position of the democracies in Europe. The Italian people, thus confronted with the choice between the concrete aid of the Marshall Plan and the pie-in-the-sky promises of communism, returned a smashing verdict against the Communists.

The Marshall Plan, which turned out to be a spectacular success, was an epochal step in both foreign policy and postwar recovery. This economic blood transfusion—altogether $10.25 billion in three years—took the Europeans off their backs and put them on their feet. It halted the westward surge of communism. It was one of the major steps in the evolution of the North Atlantic Treaty Organization (NATO). It was intervention of a sort—or counterintervention against the Communists—but intervention designed to create the economic and political conditions in which free men could make a free choice of government. Winston Churchill was not too far from the mark when he called the Marshall Plan "the most unsordid act in history." The money, to be sure, was given but it was given largely for what were deemed to be the best interests of the United States.

AIRLIFTS AND AIRWAVES

Berlin was perhaps the first critical area to suffer from Soviet resentment against the Marshall Plan. Moscow had long been disturbed by the success of the British, Americans, and French in unifying their German zones and in establishing currency reform. On June 24, 1948, therefore, the Soviets shut off all non-Russian traffic to Berlin, except by air. They evidently reasoned that America, Britain, and France, unable to supply the garrisons and populations in their sectors, would abandon the city. It would then become a rallying point for the Soviets in the unification of an all-Communist Germany.

President Truman, supported by the British, promptly and courageously refused to be run out of Berlin. In arriving at this decision, he correctly interpreted the mood of the American people. American and British airmen speedily inaugurated the Berlin airlift, through which they undertook the gigantic task of supplying not only their garrisons but the needs of some 2,500,000 people as well. "Operation Vittles," as it was called, at one time was flying in some 4500 tons of supplies a day, including coal—expensive coal.

The Berlin blockade backfired badly on Moscow. There were some ticklish scrapes with Russian fighter planes, and the peace of the world lay with the trigger fingers of Soviet airmen. But President Truman and his associates properly concluded that the Russians did not want to fight—otherwise they would have let war come then and there. The West gained in popularity with its fallen German foes, while the Soviets sank even lower. The Berlin airlift thus proved to be a stimulant to the formation of the West German Republic, and also an important step toward the North Atlantic Alliance. The Russians, pinched by a counterblockade of their zone by the West, finally agreed to end their blockade of Berlin in 1949, after about a year's trial.

Spectacular episodes meanwhile had further highlighted the pervasiveness of Soviet communism. The House Committee on Un-American Activities, which had been flushing out small-fry Communist conspirators, finally emerged with big game. It found evidence that in 1937–1938 Alger Hiss, then an official in the State Department, had betrayed important secrets to Soviet agents. After two sensational trials, Hiss was found guilty of perjury in 1950, and sentenced to a prison term of five years.

Such incidents induced the American people, despite a natural aversion to such methods, to try to match weapons with the Soviets on the propaganda front. When World War II had ended, an economy-minded Congress was giving niggardly support to an informational and cultural program, popularly known as the "Voice of America." It was designed to instruct other people in the American way of life, through radio and other agencies, and thus combat communism. As the wholesale propaganda activities of the Soviets became more blatant, and as the conviction deepened that the only way to bring the truth to the Russians and their satellites was by a short-wave radio, Congress pricked up its ears. Early in 1948 it put the "Voice of America" on a permanent basis with more adequate funds, although they were far short of what the Soviets were spending. The American short-wave radio program had serious defects, but its partial success was attested by persistent Soviet efforts to "jam" its broadcasts.

THE 12-POWER NORTH ATLANTIC PACT

The menace of Moscow elsewhere brought further noteworthy developments. In March, 1948, five nations of Western Europe—Britain, France, Belgium, the Netherlands, and Luxembourg—signed at Brussels a fifty-year defensive pact. By its terms they solemnly bound themselves to aid one another against an attack by an aggressor. The United States, as their chief economic underwriter and as a leader of the anti-Communist nations, was irresistibly drawn toward the new alliance.

Washington was in a receptive mood. In June, 1948, nearly three months after the birth of the Brussels pact, the United States Senate passed the Vandenberg resolution by the lopsided vote of 64 to 4. It affirmed American support for regional security pacts like the one recently adopted by the five European nations. With this green light plainly flashing, the State Department pressed negotiations to include the United States in the union. Moscow loudly proclaimed that Washington was weakening the United Nations (which the Soviets had already weakened), and was forming an aggressive bloc (which the Soviets had already formed by a network of treaties with their satellites). Regional security pacts conformed to both the letter and spirit of Article 51 of the UN Charter, and the proposed Atlantic alliance was clearly defensive rather than aggressive.

Representatives of twelve nations, with appropriate white-tie pageantry, finally met in Washington to sign the North Atlantic Treaty, on April 4, 1949. The charter members were the United States, Canada, Britain, France, Italy, Belgium, the Netherlands, Luxembourg, Norway, Denmark, Iceland, and Portugal. After paying their respects to the UN, they stipulated that an attack by an aggressor on one of them would be an attack on all of them. They further proclaimed that each of the other signatory nations, in the event of an assault on one member, would take "such action as it deems necessary," including "armed force." This pledge did not flatly commit the United States to war, or remove from Congress the war-declaring power. But it was a moral commitment to aid the victims of aggression for at least twenty years.

NONENTANGLEMENT BECOMES ENTANGLEMENT

The North Atlantic Pact was precedent-shattering. It was unquestionably a formal treaty of alliance, the first the United States had ever concluded in peacetime with a European power or powers. Yet such was the growing fear of the Soviet menace that this drastic departure from tradition met with widespread favor in America. The conviction was general that if World War III broke out, the republic would be sucked into it at the outset. The only sensible alternative seemed to be to attempt to avert it, as the United States had been unable or unwilling to do in 1914 and 1939, by serving notice on potential aggressors that they would have to reckon with America's might from the very outset. The loudest opposition to the alliance came from the last-ditch isolationists, from the Henry Wallaceites, and from the Communists. The leading Communist organ, the *New York Daily Worker,* branded the pact "International Murder, Inc."

The epochal North Atlantic Pact was approved by the Senate, in July, 1949, by a vote of 82 to 13. There was surprisingly little opposition. A few die-hard isolationists feared foreign entanglements, a loss of the war-declaring power of Congress, and commitments to heavy and dangerous defense expenditures. Opponents of the pact made a determined effort to relieve the United States of any obligation to rearm Western Europe, but such proposed amendments were beaten down by heavy majorities.

One presumed by-product of the North Atlantic Pact was the lifting of the Berlin blockade. Three weeks after the signing of the alliance the Soviets, in what may have been an attempt to head off American ratification, agreed tentatively to end the stoppage. The formal lifting came on May 12, 1949. The Soviets seemed less aggressive and self-assured, perhaps because of the success of the Marshall Plan, the Berlin airlift, and the Atlantic Treaty.

The threat of Russian communism had thus brought about a major revolution in American foreign policy within a few short years. The United States had reversed its Monroe Doctrine in relation to Greece by accepting the Truman Doctrine. It had forsaken nonintervention by promoting the Marshall Plan. It had tossed overboard the no-alliance tradition by signing the Atlantic Pact. It had adopted peacetime conscription and a wartime military budget. It had embarked upon all such departures with extreme reluctance but basically in response to the instinct of self-preservation. The new American policies—all defensive in their outlook—were actually authored more by the men in the Kremlin than by the men in Washington. The American people had hoped for a peaceful world after World War II, but the aggressions of the Soviets simply would not permit them to drop their guard.

4 A European View

FROM *A History of the Cold War* BY JOHN LUKACS

THE DIVISION OF EUROPE BECOMES RIGID
(TO 1949)

I

EVEN BEFORE THE END of the war Stalin alone of the Big Three remained in power. Because of the unexpected electoral victory of the British Labour Party, Churchill was replaced by Attlee during the closing days of the Potsdam Conference, where Truman had come to occupy Roosevelt's seat; soon thereafter General De Gaulle, disgusted with the new quagmire of French politics and parliaments, resigned and withdrew from public affairs. The conditions of defeated Germany and Italy were not yet auspicious for the emergence of important leaders; in China civil war was in development. Thus outside the Russian Empire the world suddenly seemed devoid of the impact of great personalities; but soon it became evident that Providence and political fortune had provided the English-speaking nations and, with them, the free world with two persons whose statesmanship proved adequate for halting the eventual spread of Russian Communist tyranny. Their integrity, bravery, and intelligence shine in retrospect through those murky years. They were Harry S. Truman and Ernest Bevin, the provincial Midwestern politician who through a stroke of fate became President of the United States and the erstwhile dock worker who became Foreign Secretary of Britain in 1945. They soon made a strong and confident impression. There were many reasons to believe that, unlike Roosevelt, the inexperienced Truman would let the State Department and its Secretaries determine the ultimate conduct of American foreign policy; but Truman, who, unlike his successor, knew from the first moment the historic traditions and necessity of strong presidential leadership, soon grasped the master wheel of the American ship of state with both hands. Meanwhile in Britain the somewhat colorless Prime Minister Attlee left to the Foreign Secretary the main task of insuring the continuity of British foreign policy in the best interests of the nation; and as early as in August 1945 Bevin's first speech in the House of Commons, direct and critical of Russian actions in Europe, dispelled the fears (or the hopes)

From *A History of the Cold War*, pp. 63–77, by John Lukacs. Copyright © 1961 by John Lukacs. Reprinted by permission of Doubleday & Company, Inc.

of those who believed that the new Labour government would go to great lengths to accommodate the Russians.

Still, the United Kingdom, victorious in principle but impoverished in essence by the war, was no longer able to maintain her far-flung imperial and political commitments in all parts of the world. The British decision to grant full independence to India, Pakistan, Burma, and Palestine was made; from 1947 on, the British flag was hauled down in many places, while elsewhere the relationship of Britain with her colonial dependencies was newly reformed to the benefit of the latter in the name of the democratic principle. Yet none of these great transformations, including the dramatic birth of the Indian and Pakistani Republics on a vast subcontinent, and not even the birth of the State of Israel, had, as yet, an important bearing on the dreadful balance of the developing cold war. It was in Greece, the historic ally of Great Britain, that the turning point was reached.

2

By early 1947 President Truman and the American government finally concluded that the United States would not further acquiesce in the Communization—either by conquest, civil war, or subversion—of any portion of Europe or the Near East that lay outside the Russian imperial sphere in Eastern Europe. The so-called Truman Doctrine, the Marshall Plan, and the Containment Policy were the three principal instruments of this historic (though, in retrospect, hardly avoidable) decision.

In February 1947 the British government informed Washington that it could not alone sustain the armed struggle of the Greek state against the growing irregular tide of Communist guerrilla armies. Without hesitation Truman assumed the burden. His Message to Congress in March 1947 called for American military aid to a Greece and Turkey threatened by Russian pressure and eventual blackmail. After some debate congressional consent was given. Forthwith American military missions and abundant supplies were sent to these Eastern Mediterranean countries. In about a year the Greek Army defeated the Communist guerrillas everywhere. The prominence of American sea power in the Eastern Mediterranean, manifested by the Sixth Fleet, remained an important factor in world affairs ever since that time.

It was evident in 1945 that American statesmen were more responsive to economic than to political arguments when it came to the distressing problems of Europe. Predicated upon the belief that Communism would primarily prosper from economic chaos, fortified by strong inclinations of American common sense as well as by traditional American institutional generosity toward poverty and distress abroad, the so-called Marshall Plan was proposed in June 1947. The United States was willing to support, in the form of goods, gifts, and easy loans, the rebuilding of the war-torn economies of Britain and Europe. The aim of the Marshall Plan was the ultimate restoration of the balance in Europe by quickly getting the weakened nations of

Western Europe to their feet again; but its purposes were broader politically and even more generous economically, since Marshall Plan Aid was offered to Eastern Europe, including Russia, too. But Stalin refused to take it; indeed, he forced his westernmost ally, the still semi-democratic republic of Czechoslovakia, to reverse its original acceptance.

His purpose of dividing Europe was now clearer than ever before. Peace Treaties were already signed with former German allies, Italy, Hungary, Rumania, Finland; but except for a few unimportant details these amounted about to a confirmation of the respective Armistice instruments signed before; moreover, Russian forces were not withdrawn from Hungary, Rumania, or Poland, where they were to guard communication lines to East Germany and Eastern Austria, pending a German and Austrian Peace Treaty. About the latter the Council of Foreign Ministers were getting nowhere during interminable debates. Through a variety of methods the Russians took ruthless advantage of the subject condition of their captive European neighbors; and in 1947 Stalin speeded up the gradual Sovietization of his prospective satellites. With crudest methods, on occasion not shunning even the open involvement of Russian police organs, the representatives of the remaining democratic forces in Hungary, Rumania, Poland, Bulgaria, and East Germany were sometimes deported, at times imprisoned, on occasion silenced, and frequently chased into Western exile. In Yugoslavia and Albania, where no Russian troops were stationed, the police control of the Communist regimes was most complete. In some of the other satellites, particularly Hungary, the unpopularity and the occasional ineptitude of local Communist satraps were still an obstacle despite the power of their Russian masters. In June 1947 the semi-democratic government of Hungary had to be transformed by force; thereafter unabashed police tactics were the main instruments for insuring Russia's mastery in Eastern Europe.

Though, except for increasingly angry protests and for individual actions of personal rescue, the Western Powers did little to intervene, Stalin's brutalities in Eastern Europe deeply affected the free world. There was, therefore, not much argument about the wisdom of the American Policy of Containment—in essence a political expression of the purpose that motivated the so-called Truman Doctrine and the Marshall Plan—formulated by the thoughtful American diplomatist George F. Kennan and first indicated in 1947 in an article under the cipher "X" in the American magazine *Foreign Affairs*. Since Communism preaches a perpetual struggle against the non-Communist world, in certain historical situations this preaching may be rationalized into ruthless expansion unless it is met by the force of determined resistance. At least in Europe, it was now the supreme interest of the United States to prohibit the further overflow of Soviet influence beyond the already swollen limits of Stalin's new Russian Empire. This is the gist of the Policy of Containment. It sums up the events of the year 1947. It also suggests the principal direction of American world policy up to the present day.

3

By 1948 the leadership of Soviet Russia and of the United States over their respective halves of Europe (and also of Korea) was an accomplished fact. While Russian domination was welcomed by but a small minority of people in the eastern, American predominance was welcomed by most people in the western half of the continent, including Germany, where events were soon to test the measure of American determination. The American response to the Russian threat in Berlin was one of the finest American hours in the history of the cold war. A sense of relief and of Western Christian unity was diffused in the hearts of millions of Europeans. It was in 1948 that the term "cold war" became popular currency (I think the phrase was Walter Lippmann's). But it was also in 1948 that the term "West" acquired a new popular historical meaning: the cold wind of the Bolshevik threat from the steppes of Asia, instead of chilling the spirit into the mortal rigor of hopeless fear, suscitated significant new fires in the European spirit; and the unity of Western Christian civilization was first felt by thinking men in Europe and America together. In the American presidential election of 1948 (the first in a series of elections that were followed all over the free world with an interest that unconsciously reflected the knowledge that here the American people were choosing the leader of the West) foreign policy played no important part; and the unexpected victory of Harry Truman, no matter what its domestic electoral sources, assured the leadership of the free world of this vigorous personality for some years to come. In Western Europe the distressing aftermath of war and poverty still prevailed; but the spirit of people, especially of the young postwar generation, compared favorably with the radical and cynical mood of disillusionment that had followed the First World War. A genuine movement toward European Unity became current; together with constructive intellectual and religious tendencies, it was also manifest in politics through the broad emergence of Christian Democratic parties whose leadership was provided by the personal excellence of De Gasperi in Italy, Adenauer in Germany, Robert Schuman in France, Figl and Raab in Austria. Partly as a consequence of these developments and partly because of the blunders of Stalin's own brutalities, the Russians now suffered their first important setbacks in Europe.

Stalin's main blunders bear the names of Czechoslovakia, Yugoslavia, and Berlin: this order is chronological as well as one of ascending importance. In February 1948, nine years after the rapacious Hitler broke his word and incorporated the remains of a cowed Czech state, not knowing that his easy subjugation of Prague was an unnecessary act whose symbolic character galvanized resistance against him in the West, Stalin acted in a similar vein. The Czechoslovak Republic, whose pliant leaders had done everything not to arouse the ire or suspicion of their mastodon Russian neighbor, was not to be given the least opportunity to maintain certain traditional contacts with the West. Even without the pressure of Russian armies, a Communist *coup d'état,* dramatized by the following suicide of the Foreign Minister, Jan Masaryk, effectively transformed Czechoslovakia into an all-out Soviet satellite. The Western Powers were not willing to intervene; but at least they took immediate steps to close their ranks and proceed with military preparations. A Western European military and political Instrument was signed in Brussels in March 1948. American military preparations in Germany increased while the still existing gradual differences in the Eastern European captive nations were being reduced to uniformity through drastic measures that indicated impatience and worrisomeness on Stalin's part. But on 28 June 1948 a Communist bulletin brought to the world the surprising news of a break between Stalin and Tito.

Few events indicate clearer the Russian national and imperialist, as distinct from Communist, motives and ambitions of Stalin than the dark (and at times almost comic) story of Russian-Yugoslav misunderstandings. In no Eastern European country was there a native Communist Party stronger than in Yugoslavia; Tito was indeed the most radical of the Communist leaders. But he was a junior partner, not a satellite; he had won his civil war, if not wholly without Russian help, at least not as a carpetbagger suppliant following behind the mighty hordes of the advancing Russian armies. Frequently Stalin preferred submissive Russian agents to steadfast Communist leaders; he grew dissatisfied with Tito's Communist South Slav nationalism from 1945 onward. As often before in history, the crudity of Russian intervention alienated those who had been her best friends in the Balkans. When his Russian agents proved unequal to the task of upsetting Tito, Stalin pronounced Communist anathema upon Yugoslavia; but his subsequent threats only united the still considerably divided Yugoslav nation behind their audacious leader, whose prestige, in contrast to Stalin's, now began to rise throughout the world.

In line with his policy to eliminate the last Western islands within his monochrome East European Empire, Stalin began to put pressure on Berlin in the spring of 1948. It will be remembered that Berlin, like Vienna, was divided into four occupational zones where for symbolic purposes all four Allies were keeping garrisons, an arrangement made in 1944 and which indeed had precedents going back to the occupation of Paris after Napoleon's fall. Unlike Vienna, where a central Austrian government resided, Berlin was not the seat of a German government. In its eastern suburbs the Russians were setting up the rudiments of an East German satellite "administration," while the West German government, after some debate, made its home in Bonn in 1949. These arrangements consequent to the practical division of Germany were not yet advanced when in May 1948 the Russians began to suspend supplies and communications between West Berlin and the Western Zones of Germany. The object of this Blockade was the starving of West Berlin into submission. It was broken from the very beginning by the resoluteness of the population in concert with Allied military determination to stand fast. Along the official highway connecting Berlin with the Western

Zone, General Clark proposed to break through the Blockade with an American military column; but President Truman chose instead to depend on American ingenuity of material supply: the famous Berlin Air Lift was created. Throughout the dark autumn and winter days of 1948 a Berlin still largely in ruins drew hope and succor from the drone of American transport planes, piloted often by the same men who but a few years before cast bombs on that same city. Almost a hundred American, British, and French airmen gave their lives for the cause of freedom in Berlin. Their sacrifice was not in vain. The Russian bluff was called. In May 1949 the Russians lifted the "Blockade."

By that time, however, outside Berlin the division of Germany had begun to ossify. In Bonn in the West and in Berlin-Pankow in the East two rival German governments were installed. The Russians were beginning to give arms to their East German police and semi-military forces, while in the West the American military emphasis grew. In 1947-48 arrangements were made for American bombers to be installed on airfields in Britain. Increasing amounts of American military equipment were given to Western European nations. The permanent establishment of American forces in Europe was finally sealed by the instrument of the North Atlantic Treaty Organization, signed in March 1949. It was already foreseeable that unless important changes were to occur in the political relations of Moscow and Washington, at least a partial rearmament of West Germany by the United States and its allies would be but a matter of time.

Thus four years after the end of the Second World War within Russian Europe all resistance was crushed; but Russian and Communist expansion seemed to have come definitely to a halt. The Russification of Stalin's new Empire proceeded with its Communization; in 1949 a Russian Army Marshal was made Defense Minister of the Polish Republic, and the elimination of even proved and radical Communists who were not known Russian agents began in the rest of the satellite countries. Still, it was not Russian but American power that swayed the destinies of most of the world. The number and the extent of American—not of Russian—military, naval, and air bases were increasing. In Europe at least, Communism failed everywhere outside the iron curtain; strong American support insured the victory of the Christian Democrats in the important Italian elections of 1948. The European balance was becoming redressed—at the cost of the abandoned Eastern European nations, but at least altogether somewhat in favor of the West. In May 1949 Molotov, whose impregnable Soviet Russian conservatism was associated with a crucial decade of Russian history and expansion, left the Soviet Foreign Ministry; Stalin appointed Vishinsky in his place. This was at least a sign of his dissatisfaction with the way Russian foreign affairs were going.

Up to that time the United States had the atomic monopoly; but now in 1949 the Russians exploded their first atomic bomb—promptly monitored by

American atomic agencies under whose aegis the plans for the construction of a Hydrogen Bomb had already begun.

4

At this point, with the first phase of the cold war closing, we must look at the ideas guiding the course of the now inimical Giant Powers of the world. Both the Russian and the American peoples were told by their leaders that the Second World War brought no real peace, that they might have to gird themselves anew for the dangers of war. This was possible without drastic interference with the domestic prosperity of America; it was not possible in Russia, where the regimen of privations continued well after the war. While the American people, relentlessly reminded of their new international responsibilities, tended more and more in an internationalist direction, Stalin's Russia became more national and isolationist than it had ever been since the Communist Revolution. By 1949 the similarities between Stalin's regime and that of Tsar Nicholas I, for example, were so obvious that pages and pages from books such as the Marquis de Custine's description of his travels in the Russia of the 1840s would apply to Stalin's Russia in the 1940s; but Americans sought the key to Soviet conduct in dogma rather than in history, in the internationalist, revolutionary, and agnostic doctrines of "Leninist" Communism, rather than in the nationalist, isolationist, and orthodox features that were emerging under Stalin, whose xenophobic, puritan, anti-Semitic terror suggested a Tsar rather than any international Communist revolutionary figure, and whose exhortations of Russian national pride had deep roots in Russian history but no source at all in Marx. The American reaction, concentrating on the dangers of international Communism rather than on the historical features of Russian aggressiveness, was of course only in part due to the myopic American intellectual tendency of taking dogmas and abstractions unduly seriously. It was also motivated by a strong domestic undercurrent, a political anti-Communist reaction against the more and more obvious falseness of wartime radical and Russophile propaganda. It was the reaction against the illusions of an intellectual and political generation now on trial: and such shocking developments as the evidence of amateur espionage practiced by people like Alger Hiss, an able young top organization man of the New Deal generation, now revealed to have been at least a Communist sympathizer, were to carry this popular anti-Communist reaction far.

Thus we find a curious and corresponding duality in American and Russian political tendencies by 1949. On one hand, the Soviet Union was, more than ever, the mighty leader of international Communism; but in reality the tendency of her tyrannical ruler was more national than international, more Russian than Communist, more isolationist than revolutionary; for example, there were (and, to some extent, there still are) two iron curtains, one separating the satellites from the rest of Europe, the other separating Russia from her Sovietized satellites, and the latter was even thicker than the first. On one hand, the United States was committing herself only to the defense of certain Western European and marginal strategic territories against the eventual armed aggression of Russia; but in reality the tendency of this American policy was becoming ideological rather than political, and world-wide rather than limited to America's admittedly vast national and Allied interests; for example, the United States, even though she had written off Eastern Europe, assumed the role of a coordinating center of Eastern European émigré political and propaganda activities, while her military intelligence organs were already involved in an underhand struggle with their Soviet counterparts throughout the whole world.

For on a vital point American intentions and purposes were not entirely clear. We have seen that while, during and even after the war, the Anglo-American purpose was, broadly speaking, the reconstruction of Europe, the Russian purpose was the division of Europe; now Europe was torn asunder, and Containment and NATO were to keep any more portions from going. But there was an important difference between NATO and Containment that has remained obscured and unresolved until the present day. The original purpose of Containment—at least in Kennan's concept—was to build up Western Europe and commit the United States in her defense so that after a while Russia's rulers would see how their aggressive behavior was leading them nowhere. Thereafter the growth of a peacefully prosperous Europe would modify the unnatural division of the continent into Russian and American military spheres, so that ultimately a mutual reduction of the more extreme Russian and American commitments and of some of their most advanced outposts could follow. These were not insubstantial speculations. They rested on political and geographical realities. In 1949 there was still an important marginal area in the middle of Europe that was not yet fully ranged within either the Russian or the American military system (indeed, until 1951 the only line where NATO's territories bordered on Russia was the short stretch of the Russian-Norwegian frontier in the extreme North). Finland was under the Russian shadow, and the Russians insisted on binding Pacts with Finland; but Stalin told the Finns that their country could remain outside the Soviet political sphere if Sweden, across the Baltic, was to stay outside NATO and the American military sphere. In 1948 neither West Germany nor, of course, Switzerland and Austria, were part of NATO; the latter, a battleground of competing intelligence agencies, was, like Germany, divided between Eastern and Western Zones but, unlike Germany, not quite hopelessly: there was a central Austrian government sitting in Vienna, recognized by both Washington and Moscow. Further to the south neither Yugoslavia nor Greece nor Turkey belonged to NATO (the latter two were then included in 1951), while it is significant that the multiple military alliances that the Russians were tying among their satellite neighbors were not extended to Albania, the only geographically isolated member of the

Soviet group of states. Thus a motley but unbroken middle European zone separated the Russian and American spheres from the Arctic to the Aegean. This was the design of Kennan, who was the head of Policy Planning in the Department of State at the time; but this subtle and reasonable policy was soon superseded by the simple and military anti-Communist concept of NATO. Where the original purpose had been the ultimate dissolution of the division of Europe and Germany, NATO was to contribute to the hardening of that division into permanence. Absorbed by this newer purpose, the necessary imagination of American statesmanship began to falter; and we shall see how thereby the character of the American state and society began to develop in a centralized and military direction.

The question, therefore, arises whether American policy had understood Stalin's ambitions well enough. It was formulated at a time when Russia in Eastern Europe proceeded with shocking brutality. Around the edge of the new Russian Empire conditions were uncertain: the Red froth bubbled in northern Greece; France and Italy seemed withering in political and economic weakness. It was of the greatest importance to halt what was considered "the Red flood" before it could trickle and flow into Italy, France, Western Europe. But was this analysis sufficiently profound? There is no sufficient evidence that Stalin in 1947–48 had planned to advance into France and Italy or that he had even contemplated the imminent victory of the Communist Parties in those countries; indeed, the evidence points to the contrary. His actions were aimed at consolidating, in some cases with frantic haste, his imperial realms in Eastern Europe; and it is quite possible that the American preoccupation with Western Europe may have suited his purposes: for thus American attention was diverted from Eastern Europe.

Perhaps it would be well to put ourselves into Stalin's position in, say, 1947. He regarded Eastern Europe as his; he also felt somewhat justified in this possession. Russia had won the war against the German invaders. Her cities were devastated, her armies bled white; with age-old Russian suspicion, Stalin was prone to underestimate the Allied contribution to the victory over Germany. Russia had carried the main brunt of the war, while the United States, without wounds, emerged as the greatest and most powerful nation of the earth. It was the Americans, now in possession of the entire Western European pastry shop, who a few years before let him have his Eastern European cake with such unconcern; why couldn't he eat it, after all? Now Stalin did not particularly contest American power: he did not challenge America's sphere; did it not seem to him, however, that the Americans were beginning to challenge *his* sphere? Always he was willing enough to go along with sphere-of-interest arrangements; he, again like Russian diplomacy in the past, was a *quid pro quo* politician of sorts. When Churchill, at Potsdam, complained about Rumania. Stalin would retort that he fulfilled their bargain by not intervening in Greece; when Churchill or Truman insisted upon Poland, Stalin answered that Poland involved Russian interests while he had not the slightest concern with how the British protected theirs in Belgium or Holland. But Churchill, that cunning old British Capitalist Enemy of Communism, at least understood him on that point; the Americans did not. Stalin did not really compete with them over Western Europe; but why were they now, after the war, two years after Yalta, getting worked up about Eastern Europe, protesting loudly about imprisoned Cardinals? He did not really challenge what to him amounted to the American domination of Western Europe; the financial assistance which Moscow had furnished the Italian Communist Party, for example, was far less than what the Americans poured into Italy before the 1948 elections. Why, then, the American meddling in Eastern Europe? Had they not won enough in the war? All of the Pacific and the Atlantic basins, plus Western and Southern Europe? With his narrow Oriental eyes looking westward from the Byzantine windows of the Kremlin, Stalin may have reasoned thus.

Thus an amused historian may say that the first few years—and perhaps even the first decade—of the Russian-American crisis over Europe might have been due to a fundamental, mutual misunderstanding: Washington presupposing that the immediate Russian aim was to upset and conquer Western Europe, Moscow presupposing that the American aim was to upset and reconquer Eastern Europe—and that both presuppositions were wrong.

Thus a cynical historian may say that Moscow and Washington did not make out so badly, after all. True, in 1945 and thereafter a more intelligent and imaginative American policy could have prevented the Russian advance into the very middle of Europe and this spared much of the cost and the toil of the cold war; true, in 1945 and thereafter less crude and brutal Russian measures in Eastern Europe would not have provoked all of these countermeasures, including NATO, and Russian influence in Europe would not have been limited to the subject satellite capitals—but the cynic may say: so what? No cold war, no American dominion over one half, and no undisputed Russian dominion over the other half of Europe. No cold war, no rigid division of Europe—ah yes, a boon to Europe it may have been: but, if so, the Russians, for instance, would not be the masters of Hungary today, and the Americans would not be able to tie an armed Germany within their military system. Still, this imaginary cynic of a historian would not be entirely right—at least not yet. For, no matter how true is the maxim that one must want the consequences of what one wants, this maxim is seldom put into practice in the affairs of men and of nations; and it is especially true in democratic ages that the discrepancy between intentions and ultimate results is great, very great indeed.